CHANGING HEARTS CHANGING LIVES

PRACTICAL IDEAS TO MAKE A DIFFERENCE IN YOUR CLASSROOM

BY JANE L. FRYAR

Edited by Arnold E. Schmidt

Contents

TO BEGIN ...

A few months after the Cuban missile crisis had burned the fear of nuclear war into my preteen mind, a roar swept through the empty church building. The floor trembled beneath my feet, and the stained glass rattled in the windows. Mom and I had come to arrange flowers on the altar for the worship service the next day. The roar convinced me—at least a few seconds—that I would worship with the angel choir in heaven the next day instead of with the church on earth in Rockwell City, Iowa.

But the bomb (or Bomb) hadn't fallen. Instead, as we learned a few hours later, a panel truck carrying a large load of dynamite had exploded three miles or so from the church building. The driver had unwisely packed blasting caps in with his explosive cargo. Fortunately, he had leaped out of the cab and into the ditch in time to avoid becoming part of the debris that rained down on a 12-foot crater in the road bed. Later that weekend I stood on the edge of that crater. I had been convinced of the power of dynamite.

I still think of that crater whenever I read Romans 1:16. The apostle Paul writes, "I am not ashamed of the Gospel, because it is the power [or *dynamite*] of God for the salvation of everyone who believes." The Greek word translated *power* is the word from which we derive the English words *dynamite, dynamo,* and *dynamic.* The Gospel carries with it tremendous power!

But that power doesn't blow craters in concrete roadbeds. It doesn't shake the earth or rattle the windows. It works quietly, sometimes almost unnoticed. Nevertheless, the results are no less dramatic, especially when you consider the hardness of human hearts and the drastic changes the Holy Spirit works as He touches and shapes by the Gospel. We once lived in darkness, blinded by our rebellion against God. Now we have, by His grace, become His children. Imagine an earthly father who would adopt a gang of criminals and take them into his home. Our heavenly Father has done just that in calling us to belong to Him and to take our place in His family.

Now that we have become the children of God, adopted into His family, the Holy Spirit works to make us just like our Big Brother, the Lord Jesus. That process—the process of discipleship—begins at the moment of our conversion and continues throughout our lives. From start to finish, the work of conversion, of transformation, of becoming more and more like Christ, is God's work. He works all these changes through His Word, His powerful—dynamic—Word.

That Word is even now at work in you. As you teach in Christ's church as Christ's representative, that Word is at work *through* you. How thrilling it is to watch as the Holy Spirit ignites the fire of saving faith in the heart of a vacation Bible school student! How wonderful to watch as the Holy Spirit nurtures the faith-relationship He has planted in the hearts of each of your Sunday school or weekday school students! What an honor our Lord has given us to take part in His holy, life-changing, heart-renovating work! What a hope belongs to us and to those we teach. Think of it! We *will* be like Jesus—in love, joy, peace, patience, kindness, goodness, faithfulness, gentleness, and self-control (Galatians 5:22–23)!

May you grow in your own discipleship as you let our Savior work through you to disciple the young people He has entrusted to your care. How does all that happen? What—specifically—will you do to facilitate that process of discipleship in your students? That's what the rest of this book is about. Read on.

> *Dear friends, now we are children of God, and what we will be has not yet been made known. But we know that when He appears, we shall be like Him, for we shall see Him as He is. (1 John 3:2)*

WHAT'S THE BIG IDEA?

TRANSFORMATION

1

Teaching for a Change in Church

"What's the big idea?" Maybe you asked yourself that question as you read the title of this chapter. "Hasn't the church always taught? We have Sunday school, vacation Bible school, midweek classes, confirmation instruction, Bible classes. What do you mean, 'teaching for a change' "?

Or maybe different thoughts are cascading through your mind. Maybe you're thinking, "I want my teaching to make a difference in the lives of my students. I see some changes sometimes. But I'm not sure I teach with change in mind. Can I do that? Does God want me to do that? And even if He does, what kinds of change do you mean?"

HOW DOES CHANGE HAPPEN?

We want to examine ways God might use us as change agents in the lives of our students. That's the main topic of this book. But first we need to look at how spiritual growth—growth in discipleship—happens in human hearts. To do that, we need to remember God's "goals and objectives" for His children. What does He hope to accomplish in us?

Your heavenly Father always has yearned, planned, and worked toward a single goal—creating an eternal family and placing you (yes, you!) in it:

[In His love] He chose us—actually picked us out for Himself as His own—in Christ before the foundation of the world; that we

9

should be holy (consecrated and set apart for Him) and blameless in His sight, even above reproach, before Him in love (Ephesians 1:4, Amplified Bible).

You know how Adam and Eve spoiled God's original plan for accomplishing that goal. But human sin did not change God's mind. He still wanted you (yes, you!) in His family. His biggest idea—His greatest dream since the Garden of Eden—has been our *transformation.*

God wants to give all human beings, and especially you (yes, you!) the joy of living in His "forever family" as His unique and precious child. He wants you to belong to Him, to receive His unlimited love, and to live in relationship with Him and His other children. He wants all our lives knitted together in a flawless seam of love.

You know how our Lord acted "while we were still sinners" (Romans 5:8) to make His eternal dream a possibility. The words roll off our lips so easily. They flow across my computer screen with the speed of words I've typed a thousand times before. But think how these truths have changed our lives—transformed your life, my life, individually and personally!

Christ died for our sins according to the Scriptures, that He was buried, that He was raised on the third day according to the Scriptures, ...

Christ has indeed been raised from the dead, the firstfruits of those who have fallen asleep. For since death came through a man, the resurrection of the dead comes also through a man. For as in Adam all die, so in Christ all will be made alive. But each in his own turn: Christ, the firstfruits; then, when He comes, those who belong to Him. (1 Corinthians 15:3–4; 20–23).

SO WHAT AND NOW WHAT?

What does the death of a Jewish teacher two thousand years ago have to do with us? Simply this. Christ died for our sins, in our place. His death should have been mine—and yours. His cross should have been mine—and yours. His agony should have been mine—and yours. And all of that eternally.

Christ Jesus loves us so much that He paid the ultimate price for us; He died in our place. But He didn't stay dead. Neither the heavy stone, the squad of Roman soldiers, or Pontius Pilate's official seal could hold Christ captive. He walked out of His tomb a free man. He broke the shackles of sin—our sin. He crushed the ancient serpent's head, defeating our arch-enemy. He pried death's bony fingers off our throats.

Because Christ died, we live. We live right now, and we live forever. Satan can no longer hold us as fearful hostages to sin and death. We have become the children of God Himself. Our ransom has been paid in full. The "gruesome threesome"—sin, Satan, and death—can no longer suck us back into despair. We're no longer hopeless and helpless. We have a Savior. Christ died for our sin. *Christ died for our sin!*

How can love that deep just lie still in some stagnant pool in a dark corner of our hearts? Once we've received love like that, how can it help but change the way we think, the way we live? Answer: It *must* make a difference. And it *does* make a difference.

CONCRETE THEOLOGY

If we believe in Christ, the Holy Spirit has already planted the life of Christ in our hearts, and His life—eternal life—has begun its work in you (yes, you!) as in each of God's sons and daughters. As God's Spirit planted that life in you, He began the life-long process of *transformation:*

> For those God foreknew He also predestined to be conformed to the likeness of His Son, that He might be the firstborn among many brothers (Romans 8:29).

This process of "conformation," of transformation, goes on throughout our lives:

> He who began a good work in you will carry it on to completion until the day of Christ Jesus (Philippians 1:6).

And God has promised to finish the process He has begun. This will happen the day we go home to live with Him in the heavenly home:

Dear friends, now we are children of God, and what we will be has not yet been made known. But we know that when He appears, we shall be like Him, for we shall see Him as He is (1 John 3:2).

The Bible calls Christ "the firstborn from among the dead" (Colossians 1:18), the "firstborn among many brothers" (Romans 8:29). Through His cross Jesus made it possible for us to be His brothers and sisters, to bear the family name "Christian," to walk through physical death and away from eternal death unscathed. Christ went first; we follow Him.

Easter is ...

Spring

        and eggs

        and grass growing in sidewalk cracks

    And life is new

        and Christ is born

    Never again to die.

Birds

        and dew

        and, hey, tulips live through winter

    And life is new

        and I'm reborn

    And I will live forever!

The power of life. In spring we see it everywhere. A single blade of grass or two, once imbedded in concrete, eventually will break a sidewalk apart. Christ's life, growing within us, will eventually crack and then break apart even the hardest, most encrusted places of our hearts.

Christ's life in us continually transforms our hearts so that they become places of confidence and peace, places from which love flows. Christ's life in us seeps through every nook and cranny of our hearts. It warms and softens those hearts toward God and toward other people. Little by little we become on the outside what God has already made us on the inside—His righteous children.

As we study this process of salvation, especially as the New Testament writers describe it, we see its several facets. In some passages, the Bible says we *have been saved* (Ephesians 2:8); in other places it says we *are being saved* (1 Corinthians 1:18); and in still other places it promises we *will be saved* (Mark 16:16).

First, from God's eternal point of view, our salvation is already an accomplished fact. He sees us as redeemed, holy, and perfectly blameless. From this perspective, the vantage point of eternity, we "have been saved."

Second, from our vantage point here in time, God's work of salvation is in process. We see ourselves from inside our own skin as people who "are being saved." We experience minute-by-minute our need for the Holy Spirit's continuing work in our lives.

Third, from the vantage point of the Spirit carrying on His sanctifying work until the day we go home to live with Jesus in heaven, we "will be saved." God's work in us will be completed on the day our Savior takes us home and introduces us in person to His heavenly Father and all His holy angels. We will explore the methods the Spirit uses in His process of "conforming us into the image of the Son" in a later chapter. For now, remember that the Spirit works through some seemingly ordinary things—His Word; the water of Baptism connected with His Word; and the bread and wine we receive in Holy Communion together with Christ's body and blood—again intimately tied to His Word.

MAKING DISCIPLES

The process of salvation, of "conformation to the image of Christ," transforms us. This transformation is God's work in us from beginning to end, and not something we drum up inside ourselves in our own strength. Even so, our Lord has chosen to involve us. He invites us into partnership with Himself. He has commissioned us as His ambassadors here on earth, to serve as His hands, His feet, His voice. Through us He touches lives with His Word of confrontation and comfort, Law and Gospel. Perhaps you know Matthew 28:19–20 well enough to recite it from memory:

Go and make disciples of all nations, baptizing them in the name of the Father and of the Son and of the Holy Spirit, and teaching them to obey everything I have commanded you. And surely I am with you always, to the very end of the age.

We sometimes call these words of the Lord Jesus our "missionary marching orders." We understand our Savior to say that we are to carry the Good News of the salvation He has won to those who do not know Him. And the words certainly do mean that. But they also refer to the on-going work of discipling He wants to continue to do in the lives of our brothers and sisters in the faith.

Salvation has several facets, and so does discipleship. In one sense, God's people are disciples from the moment the Holy Spirit brings us to faith in Christ. God has declared it so.

In another sense, God's process of discipling us will continue throughout our earthly lives. God has made us disciples. We are disciples already. And we are being discipled—becoming more like our Teacher—as we use the power He provides in Word and Sacrament to grow in our relationship with Him. This is His dream for us and for each individual student in the classes we teach.

How remarkable God's patience as He accomplishes His transforming work in our lives! How remarkable too that He gives us a part in His work of discipling others! Of course, the Holy Spirit can—and has—worked with people solely through His written Word. This happened as they faced the horror of solitary confinement or isolation from other believers for one reason or another. But God ordinarily involves other people in the discipleship process—people who touch our lives in meaningful ways.

Relationship. It's key to discipleship goals and methods.

STOP

Stop for a moment here. Think about these questions and jot down some of your thoughts before you go on.

Which two or three individual Christians stand out in my mind as having been used by God to disciple me?

What did these people do that made a difference in my walk with the Lord Jesus?

TWO F'S, TWO A'S

A key passage to understanding God's discipleship goals for all His people comes from the Old Testament book of Psalms:

> *[The Lord] decreed statutes for Jacob*
> *and established the law in Israel,*
> *which He commanded our forefathers*
> *to teach their children,*
> *so the next generation would know them,*
> *even the children yet to be born,*
> *and they in turn would tell their children.*
> *Then they would put their trust in God*
> *and would not forget His deeds*
> *but would keep His commands.*
> *They would not be like their forefathers—*
> *a stubborn and rebellious generation*
> *whose hearts were not loyal to God. (Psalm*
> 78:5–8)

Do you see four discipleship goals in the last few lines of this passage?

Faith. God's people will "put their trust in [Him]." This refers to the faith-relationship that stands as the firm foundation for all spiritual growth. God wants us to trust Him. He invites and even commands us to do so. He has proved Himself trustworthy by keeping His promise to send His Son as our Savior from sin. We can trust Him with "the present life"—the struggles and problems of our everyday lives right now—as well as with "the life to come" (1 Timothy 4:8). Growth in Christian discipleship involves growth in both dimensions of trust.

Facts. God's people will "not forget His deeds." The Christian faith is grounded in the fact that God has intervened in human history. In fact, God entered human history in the person of Jesus Christ. All other human religions could and probably would continue to influence people even if historians could somehow prove that the leaders who founded those belief systems had never really lived. But St. Paul makes it perfectly clear that Christianity rises or falls with the answer to one factual question: Did Jesus Christ get up off the cold slab in Joseph's tomb that once supported His dead body? *If Christ has not been raised, our preaching is useless and so is* *your faith. ... If Christ has not been raised, your faith is futile; you are still in your sins (1 Corinthians 15:14, 17).* Growth in Christian discipleship involves growth in cognitive, intellectual understanding of the facts of the Christian faith.

Actions. God's people will "keep His commands." The reformers often stated the relationship between faith and a godly life this way: *Faith alone saves, but faith is never alone.* Or even more simply: *Faith works.* We can expect that our relationship with God will show itself in our lives. We're being transformed, from the inside out. When a contractor remodels a house internally, the changes may not show from the street. The neighbors may not know what's going on. But when the Holy Spirit remodels us, others begin to notice. They see the love, joy, peace, patience, kindness, goodness, faithfulness, gentleness, and self-control He is developing on the interior of our lives. Growth in Christian discipleship involves growth in Christ-like actions.

Attitudes. Finally, the psalmist addresses attitudinal goals. He does this by citing a negative example: ancient Israel. Their Lord had rescued them from slavery in Egypt; He had cared for them for 40 long years in the wilderness during which time He saw to it that they had food to eat and water to drink (no small feat in the desert through which they travelled); He had even kept their sandals from wearing out; He had provided a pillar of fire that lit up their nights and drove away their fears, and the cloudy pillar that gave them shade from the desert sun. Despite all this, the people became "a stubborn and rebellious generation whose hearts were not loyal to God." Again and again they forgot God's goodness. Again and again they dug in their heels and refused to trust, to obey, to thank or praise Him. Again and again their disloyalty broke God's heart. Growth in Christian discipleship includes growth in godly attitudes, attitudes of love and loyalty to Christ and to His family, His Church.

Faith. Facts. Actions. Attitudes. Growth in Christian discipleship involves all four dimensions.

Think About This

Use this diagram to evaluate your own discipleship in each of the four discipleship dimensions you just read about. Our Lord urges—

even commands—us to examine ourselves and our faith-life (2 Corinthians 13:5), so ask Him to help you be as honest as you can. Acknowledge both the transformation He has already worked by His grace and your need for further growth.

a. Put an × on the continuum labelled "faith" between 0 and 10. 0 means you trust God 0% of the time with 0% of your needs; 10 means you enjoy 100% assurance 24 hours of every day that God will take care of your every need.

b. Put an × on the continuum labelled "facts" between 0 and 10. 0 means you cannot name even one of Jesus' earthly parents and do not know what the Apostles' Creed is; 10 means you could teach seminary courses in Bible history and Christian doctrine.

c. Put an × on the continuum labelled "actions" between 0 and 10. 0 means that as far as you're concerned, God gave "The Ten Suggestions" on Mt. Sinai, and 24 hours each day you have a better idea; 10 means your quotients of love, joy, peace, patience, kindness, goodness, faithfulness, gentleness, and self-control are approaching those of the angel Gabriel.

d. Put an × on the continuum labelled "attitudes" between 0 and 10. 0 means ancient Israel could have learned a few things from you about how to develop bad attitudes; 10 means that if everyone in the Christian church had your attitude toward God and toward your brothers and sisters in the faith, no one could tell the difference between the church on earth and the church in heaven.

e. Now use a ruler to connect the dots.

- Is your drawing symmetrical? Or skewed in one or more dimensions?

- Is the figure as large as you would like? Larger than you expected? Smaller?

- As you look at the diagram, for what would you like to thank your Lord? Is there anything you would like to confess? What would you like to ask Jesus to continue to change?

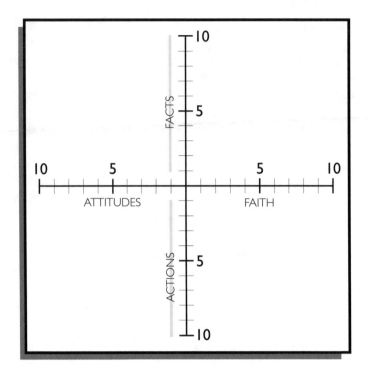

Do This

Use the diagram below to help yourself evaluate the emphasis you place on each dimension of Christian discipleship in your teaching. Think back over what actually happened in your classroom the past three or four weeks. Then mark the continuums this way:

a. Put an × on the continuum labelled "faith" between 0 and 10. 0 means the Holy Spirit could use no activity or discussion you've led in the past month to encourage and empower the students to trust in God; 10 means your students have grown in trust so much that each of them continually encourages you and one another toward a deeper trust in our Lord.

b. Put an × on the continuum labelled "facts" between 0 and 10. 0 means none of your activities the past few weeks would have given any student any kind of new factual information about salvation history or Christian doctrine; 10 means that as a result of all they've learned, your students are now equipped with the factual knowledge they would need to teach seminary courses in Bible history and Christian doctrine.

c. Put an × on the continuum labelled "actions" between 0 and 10. 0 means your class never discusses the implication of the Bible lesson for their behavior in everyday life and you have never done any kind of project together to practice showing the love of Jesus to others; 10 means that each week you and your students work together to invent new ways to show Christ-like love based on the implications of that week's Bible lesson and that you spend some time each month actually doing service projects together.

d. Put an × on the continuum labelled "attitudes" between 0 and 10. 0 means you don't believe the church is the right place to address people's attitudes; 10 means that if everyone in the Christian church had the attitudes your students show toward God and toward one another, someone walking into your classroom could not tell the difference between your classroom and the church in heaven.

e. Now use a ruler to connect the dots.

- Is the figure that results symmetrical? Or skewed in one or more dimensions?

- Is the figure as large as you would like? Larger than you expected? Smaller?

- As you look at the diagram, for what would you like to thank your Lord? What would you like to ask Jesus to continue to change?

- What does the diagram suggest about the next lesson plan you will write? What will you keep the same? What might you consider changing?

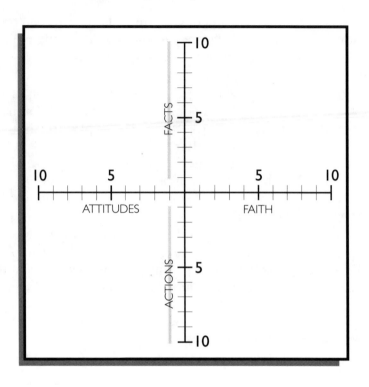

WHAT'S THE BIG IDEA?

TEACHERS AS CATALYSTS

2

Change Agents

"In the event of an emergency, the overhead doors will open and an oxygen mask will drop down. Place the mask firmly over your mouth and nose and breathe normally. Then secure the elastic strap behind your head. First secure your own mask; then help anyone traveling with you who may need assistance."

I hate the smell of jet fuel. The noise and bustle at major airports make me nervous. I start to sweat when I hear the thud of the landing gear as it retracts or deploys; I momentarily believe we've hit some odd bit of airborne debris that has managed to poke a hole in the fuselage—a hole that will soon pitch the plane into a nosedive straight to earth. And has anyone ever actually *used* one of those flimsy seat cushions as a "flotation device" anyhow? If the oxygen mask has dropped down from the door overhead, the last thing I'm going to be able to do is to "breathe normally."

Even so, the last line of the flight attendant's speech has always impressed me as very practical advice—for life outside the airplane cabin (and I pray that's the *only* place I'll ever get to use it): "First secure your own mask; then help anyone traveling with you who may need assistance."

It can sound selfish to take care of your own need for oxygen first. But no one being asphyxiated will be able to think clearly enough to help someone else. Both helper and helpee will likely black out.

Similarly, it may sound unnecessary or selfish to begin a discussion of the how-tos of Christian education with a chapter on the teacher's own personal spiritual life and growth. But in reality, if you're not breathing deeply of the fresh grace our Lord offers, you

23

won't have the spiritual strength you need to help someone else. No, not even small children who are traveling through life on the seat beside you.

CATALYSTIC CONVERSION

Your car probably has a catalytic converter. As the exhaust gases from your engine pass through it, they are changed from pollutants into simple oxygen, nitrogen, water vapor, and carbon dioxide— harmless gases that normally make up the air on Planet Earth.

The catalyst is key. It speeds up a chain of reactions that would ordinarily take a lot longer. If the exhaust reached the air un-changed—unconverted—they would damage the environment. But because the pollutants are changed inside the catalytic converter before they can escape into the atmosphere, the air remains clean, breathable.

Chemists have learned to use catalysts to make the manufac-ture of many everyday products practical. To anyone but a chemist, catalysts seem almost magical. They speed up processes that would ordinarily take much, much longer. Despite the important part they play in the reaction, they retain their helpful properties; after the reaction ends, the catalyst is left behind. It can do its job again and again without being used up.

You, a teacher in a Christian classroom, function in many ways as a human catalyst. By God's grace and as He enables you:

- You play an active, important part in the transformation, "conformation" process God has initiated in the lives of your students, the process of discipleship we talked about in chapter 1.

- You make it possible for that process to happen more thor-oughly and more quickly than it would without you.

- When your part in the transformation process is finished in the hearts and lives of individual students, they move on; you remain behind, enabled by our Lord to take part in His process of transforming another group of His people.

Before You Go On

What three or four people can you identify who have been spiritual catalysts for you, gifts from God in helping you grow in your own life of discipleship?

_____

_____

_____

_____

What did these people do to stimulate your spiritual growth?

_____

_____

_____

_____

WHAT DOES IT TAKE TO BE A CATALYST?

Not just any old chemical will do in a car's catalytic converter. Most converters contain a specific mixture of three elements—platinum, palladium, and rhodium. Pick any other elements from the Periodic Chart you stared at during all those hours of high school chemistry, and they won't work. The reaction simply won't proceed. Not even silver or gold will do. Rhodium. Palladium. Platinum. Period.

If your congregation has asked you to teach in one of its educational agencies, and if the Holy Spirit has affirmed that calling in the quiet place in your heart where He speaks to you about His specific will for you, then you can be assured that your Lord wants to use you (yes, you!) as a spiritual catalyst in the lives of your students. By His grace, you will play a unique part in their growing discipleship.

Whether you believe it or not, whether you feel like it or not, no one else can do quite the same things God has equipped you to do in their lives. No one else will approach the process in quite the same way you will. Not even that "gold-plated" super-teacher down the hall you admire so much. Not even that "five-silver-star" educator whose experience and knowledge you envy. You are uniquely equipped by the Holy Spirit Himself! What a powerful, encouraging thought!

You may yearn for more ability, more Bible knowledge, or more transformation in your own faith-life, and doubtless your Lord wants to help you attain them. Nevertheless, He wants to use you—you—to help others grow, even while you are growing yourself. You are His chosen catalyst, His agent of change, given as a gift to His people. Given specifically to the students who sit in front of you each Sunday morning or Wednesday evening.

CHOSEN AND EQUIPPED

Yes, your Lord has chosen you and me. Why? We could scarcely summarize His purposes for us more precisely or concisely than Luther did in his explanation of the Second Article:

That I may be His own and live under Him in His kingdom and serve Him in everlasting righteousness, innocence, and blessedness.
From Luther's Small Catechism copyright © 1986 CPH.

The fact that God has chosen us, both for His family and for His service, does not cancel our need for additional preparation. Instead, it motivates us to grow in our own discipleship so that we can serve our King and our brothers and sisters in Christ's kingdom in ever more powerful ways.

We can count on Christ to keep on discipling us, transforming us into His image, even as we can count on Him to equip us to be catalysts for change in the spiritual lives of our students. He has promised to do this.

Still, spiritual growth does not happen accidentally. The Holy Spirit does not come to us floating through the atmosphere like some kind of heavenly fog. He could do that, but He has instead chosen to use means—channels, conduits—through which to touch our hearts and transform our lives. We call these the means of grace. And we believe that God acts through them in powerful ways.

These means of grace include His Word, Baptism, and the Lord's Supper. Familiar tools for spiritual growth. In fact, maybe a bit too familiar. Too familiar in the sense that we can so easily take them for granted—believe they work and then neglect to use them for days, weeks, or even months on end.

Or maybe we do use them regularly, but in less than fully helpful ways. Work through the following inventory to evaluate how fully you are currently using the power God makes available to you in His means of grace. Be honest with yourself. Remember that we all need to grow in our devotional lives. But also keep in mind that the Holy Spirit has been at work in your heart and life. Be sure to give Him credit for the work He has already done.

Put a cross in the blanks next to the statements that, by God's grace, accurately describe your devotional life most of the time.

Put a question mark next to the statements that summarize thoughts that are new or challenging to you; ideas you would like to think about some more and possibly incorporate into your devotional life someday.

Put a star next to statements that describe habits you would like very much to incorporate into your devotional life immediately. (Note: If you star more than two or three items, you may find yourself in over your head and tempted to give up. Remember, God's transforming work in you will take a lifetime. So begin wherever you are at the present time, pray for the Holy Spirit's direction and power, and then choose a few areas that need attention.

_____ I attend worship services each week.

_____ I read my Bible for personal encouragement at least five days a week.

_____ I go to God in prayer, confessing my sins and receiving His assurance of forgiveness every day.

_____ I come to the Lord's Table as often as I can, not to earn His favor or to impress others, but to receive His forgive ness and power.

_____ Each day, I remind myself of my Baptism and that God has chosen me and adopted me as His very own child.

_____ When I read the Bible, I read it as God's letter of love to

me, not as a book of rules I should follow so that I can be
a better example or that God will love me more.

_____ When I come to God's house to worship Him with other
believers, I ask the Holy Spirit to prepare and open my
heart to praise Him, to receive more of His transforming
love, and to keep me from "worshiping" from a rut of rou
tine.

_____ I "pray God's promises" from the Scriptures back to Him,
reminding Him what He has said He will do and praising
Him for His answers to my requests even before I see them
materialize.

If we're going to teach for change in church, if we're going to
serve as spiritual catalysts in the lives of our students, we need to be
growing—by God's grace—in our own discipleship. We need to
set intentional priorities. We need to "seek first [Christ's] kingdom
and [Christ's] righteousness," knowing that we will then find enough
time and energy to do all those other things in our lives that need
doing too.

Still, it's as true for us as for our students—God Himself must
make the changes in us. We have zero power to transform ourselves. We cannot conform ourselves to the image of Christ. Our
lives won't look like His as we strive to make them so—no matter
how hard we work at it.

Trying hard to motivate ourselves to study the Scriptures and
to obey God's commands won't work. Pulling on our own boot-
straps in an effort to yank ourselves out of habit sins will prove
useless every time—no matter how hard we pull. Urging our students to try harder to be good, to obey their parents, to pay attention in class, or to be kind to one another will never transform them
into more Christ-like people. Never. Not even a little bit.

Does God want us to "be good and do right"? Absolutely. He
knows it's the only way to live a fulfilled and fulfilling life. But His
process for getting us from where we are today to that place He
would like us to be is not what we'd expect. In fact, if He had not
revealed it to us in His Word and in His Son, we never would have
guessed it on our own.

What *is* that process? The next chapter explains it.

Think About This

Have you ever wondered, "Who am *I* to think I have anything to give the 'King's Kids' who sit under my teaching each week?" The words of 2 Corinthians 3:1–4:18 can comfort and encourage teachers in Christ's church when we wonder about that question.

- Read these two chapters in your own Bible. Underline the verses you find especially meaningful.

- Does anyone else who teaches in your congregation need encouragement right now? How could you share one or two of the verses you underlined to encourage them?

Do This

Since God is the only one who can make the seed of His Word sprout and grow in our own hearts and in the hearts of our students (1 Corinthians 3:5–7), we need to come to Him regularly and often in prayer. Some teachers in the church find it helpful to have a prayer partner for themselves and their class. Could you ask someone—perhaps even someone who is homebound and cannot easily participate in the ministries of your congregation—to pray regularly for you and your class?

Each week, contact your prayer partner. Share specific prayer needs (but take care to protect the confidentiality of your students). Let yourself be vulnerable enough to share your own needs too. Together keep track of your requests and of God's answers, and remember to thank Him for the good things He is doing.

FROM THE FILES

Case History—Eric

Every teacher in the congregation dreaded the day Eric would show up for class. Even the pastor found his stomach churning when Eric walked through the front door of the church. For two years Eric attended midweek class. He came sporadically, and I quickly learned that if Eric was there I might as well throw half of my lesson plan overboard; we'd never get to it.

I worried, thought, prayed, and fumed about how to get through to Eric, and I'm afraid I too often blew up at him over one infraction or another. He wasn't mean—just thoughtless and disinterested. Still, he kept coming back.

A few years after Eric's confirmation, I heard through the congregation's grapevine that Eric had been arrested for trying to buy drugs while on a field trip with his high school class. He did some time in a juvenile detention center. After that, I lost track of him.

Five or so years later, I looked up from my plate of fried chicken at a church picnic and into Eric's eyes and still-freckled face. He asked me to stand up so he could hug me and introduce me to his friends. "This is my teacher," he said. "I gave her a lot of grief. But she kept caring about me. Now that I know Jesus, I know why she did. I'm really glad she took the time. But I still think she shoulda whacked me for lots of the smart-mouthing I did."

Is there an "Eric" in your class right now—someone whose heart seems sealed up tight against the work of the Holy Spirit? How would you describe your "Eric"?

How would you describe your attitude toward that student?

Why can you have hope, even for those students who seem not to care about the things of God?

How can that hope change your attitude toward discipling them?

Key Thought: Only the Holy Spirit can transform the human heart. He calls us to faithfulness in Word and example, while He retains the responsibility for the results of our witness.

WHAT'S THE BIG IDEA?

ALL BY GRACE

3

Changing Hearts, Changing Lives

Dwight L. Moody once observed, "Most believers have just enough Christianity to make them miserable." Maybe you've been there. I know I have. At times like that, we know enough about the Scriptures to identify attitudes and actions in our lives that fail to honor God. We know we need to change. But we do not understand how to plug into the power of God to change. Or we fail to do so for one reason or another. Misery. It's the unavoidable result.

All those who know Jesus Christ as their Savior want to be like Him. And in our heavenly Father's eyes, we already are! As St. Paul says of us, "If anyone is in Christ, he is a new creation; the old has gone, the new has come!" (2 Corinthians 5:17).

 Key Terms

Justification: God's act of grace in declaring us not guilty—righteous—before Him because of Christ's death on the cross for our sins.

Sanctification: God's act of grace in working in us those thoughts, attitudes, and actions that are pleasing in His sight and that grow out of saving faith.

Our Lord has not called us to be His own so we can live lives of misery. He has not destined us to frustration. Rather, He has called us to a life of fruitfulness. He wants us to grow as His disciples. He wants us to know the joy that comes as we bear abundant fruit, and He makes lives of fruitfulness possible for us.

To move from frustration to fruitfulness, though, we must understand and consistently apply two key doctrines of Holy Scripture—Law and Gospel. Only as the Holy Spirit counsels and encourages us through His Word with both Law and Gospel can we grow consistently toward Christ-likeness. Then, and only then, will we find our own personal discipleship exciting and fulfilling. Then, and only then, can we serve as catalysts for spiritual growth in the lives of our students.

LAW AND GOSPEL IN JUSTIFICATION

Not all Christians use the terms Law and Gospel. But every true Christian grasps the difference between Law and Gospel for justification.

The Law thunders its "thou shalts" and "thou shalt nots." Written in our hearts, the Law dogs our steps. It demands of us perfect thoughts, perfect words, perfect deeds. It hounds us, holding us to standards no sinful human being can attain. It requires perfection. One hundred percent obedience.

When we fail—and we do fail!—the Law shouts accusations at us. It exposes each of our sins in wretched detail. It forces us to recognize that with our own power we cannot resist sin.

The Law goes further still. It paints a picture of God's judgment, of His wrath. It warns us of the punishment we have earned by our rebellion. It dooms us. For now. For ever.

The Gospel, on the other hand, demands nothing from us. It comes to us as a kind invitation from our loving Father. It comforts us with the truth of what our dear Lord Jesus has done for us on the cross. It tells us that God has given us Jesus' very own righteousness to replace our own tattered attempts to be good enough. The Gospel presents Christ as our substitute, the one who drank the bitter wine of God's wrath to the dregs—for us.

The Gospel goes further. It promises that God gives the free gift of eternal life to all those who believe in Jesus. The Gospel declares us free from sin, from death, and from Satan's power. We need not—we cannot—do anything to earn all this. This freedom comes to us without any effort or merit on our part—solely as a free gift of God's grace.

The Holy Spirit gives us faith to believe the promises of the Gospel. Thus we escape the threats of the Law. By God's grace we become the Father's new creation. By His grace we become His heirs, members of His family, part of His royal priesthood. And, yes, our Teacher, also confers on us the title "disciple."

Almost any fourth grader can learn to tell the difference between Law and Gospel. It seems simple—childishly so. But do not let Satan or your own flesh deceive you. In his Thesis III, Dr. C. F. W. Walther states:

> To distinguish properly between Law and Gospel is the most diffi-cult and exalted skill of Christians and theologians, a skill that only the Holy Spirit teaches in the school of experience.

Walther then goes on to comment:

> Some of you may perhaps think, "What? Is that really true? ... Can this be the most difficult skill? I have mastered it."

> But ... it is the practical application which is so difficult that no human being can achieve it on the basis of his own reflection. The Holy Spirit must teach it to us in the school of experience.[1]

We probably struggle little, if at all, as we think intellectually about the concepts of Law and Gospel. The slippery work begins as we apply these truths, especially as we apply them in our own lives and in the lives of our students, in the area of sanctification.

THE LAW'S ROLE IN SANCTIFICATION

Many Christians view their growth in discipleship as a kind of spiritual do-it-yourself project. They freely admit they can do nothing to save themselves. But they believe that they must somehow sanctify themselves. Once they have received God's free and full forgiveness, they assume they must get busy and try hard to be good, to be like Jesus. Sometimes we use the term *moralism* to describe this behavior and attitude.

Christians caught up in the trap of moralism often use terms such as *try,* or *try hard,* or *try harder.* They set the Law in place like a ladder, grit their teeth, and begin to climb, rung-by-rung, using their own power, toward Christ-likeness. Immediately, the basis of their relationship with Christ slips from grace to a concern with performance. They focus on their own efforts rather than on their Savior and what He has accomplished for us. They forget or ignore one fact: God's Law never says *try;* God's Law says *do!*

Believers who insist on climbing the ladder of the Law under their own power cannot help but fall on the sharp rocks of the Law's demands time after time. Sooner or later they begin to believe that something is wrong with their faith. They carry a heavy, heavy burden of guilt. They feel inadequate. They begin to wonder how God could possibly love them. Eventually many give up. They conclude that growing up in Christ is impossible. They may even look with suspicion at believers around them who talk about spiritual growth and who desire to produce a "harvest of righteousness" for their Lord (Hebrews 12:11; James 3:18).

On the other hand, some believers who try hard to clamber up the ladder of the Law trick themselves into believing they have actually made it to the top—at least far enough toward heaven anyway so that God will have to take them the rest of the way. They fool themselves into thinking they have their lives together. They have kept God's Law—or at least the most important parts of it.

Like the Pharisees of the New Testament, these ladder-climbers feel a bit superior to those of us who still slog along in the swamp of temptation. They look down with pity on those of us who sometimes slip into the quicksand of disobedience.

No matter how diligently we search, we will never find any Scriptural evidence that God gave us His Law as a ladder. Rather, His Word describes the Law as a mirror (James 1:22–25). A mirror makes it possible for us to see the smudges on our face. But no one in her right mind ever tried to wash her face with a mirror!

God's Law can point out our sin. Also, the Law, like a compass, can point us in the right direction as we follow our Savior down the road of discipleship. But the Law cannot help us get rid of sin—

its guilt or its power. The Law cannot give us the desire or the strength we need to pick up our feet and walk along the path of discipleship. The Law is powerless to produce the fruit of sanctification in the lives of Christ's disciples.
Only the Gospel can do that!

THE GOSPEL'S ROLE IN SANCTIFICATION

God justifies us by grace. What a marvelous truth! But equally marvelous is this: God also sanctifies us by grace!

We will never become good by trying hard. And (note this well!) the students who sit under our teaching will never grow in their discipleship by trying hard, either. God has already declared us good, holy, righteous. The Holy Spirit leads us to believe that. Then He begins the process of transformation by which we live out the new life He has placed within our hearts.

This is not just theological double-talk. It's not some religious mumbo-jumbo. It makes a tremendous difference in how we see ourselves and our Lord! This truth can revolutionize a believer's life. Think of it! God wants to carry the burden of our spiritual growth. If we are honest with ourselves, we know that we could never carry it anyway. It's so heavy it would crush us in an instant.

But if God does not expect us to "try hard" to obey Him, then what does He expect? Are we merely robots whom He programs? Of course not. Then how exactly does sanctification happen? How do we grow to become more like Jesus?

THE "R" WORD

The answer to all our *how* questions lies in a process, the process of repentance. As with everything else in our life with God, this process centers in the cross. It centers in the death and resurrection of Christ Jesus. It centers in the covenant God made with each of us in our Baptism, the covenant of grace. The apostle Paul explains it in detail:

> *What shall we say, then? Shall we go on sinning so that grace may increase? By no means! We died to sin; how can we live in it any longer? Or don't you know that all of us who were baptized into*

37

Christ Jesus were baptized into His death? We were buried with Him through Baptism into death in order that, just as Christ was raised from the dead through the glory of the Father, we too may live a new life. If we have been united with Him like this in His death, we will certainly also be united with Him in His resurrection. For we know that our old self was crucified with Him so that the body of sin might be done away with, that we should no longer be slaves to sin—because anyone who has died has been freed from sin. (Romans 6:1–7)

THE PROCESS OF REPENTANCE

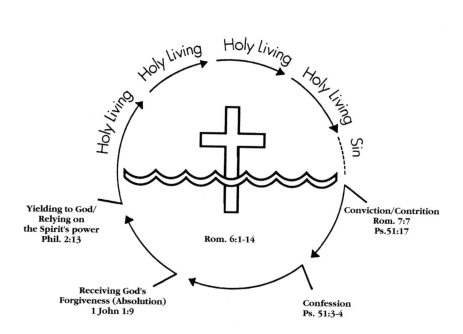

Copyright © CPH 1990, 1992. Reproduced from *Go and Make Disciples; The Goal of the Christian Teacher.*

A Sunday school teacher once asked her class, "What is the first thing we must do in order to be forgiven?"

One boy's hand shot up immediately. "Sin!" he shouted.

And of course, he was perfectly correct. The process of repentance begins as the Holy Spirit uses His Law to convict us of a specific sin and to produce true contrition within our hearts.

As the apostle Paul once discussed contrition, he sought to help his readers distinguish between "godly sorrow" and "worldly sorrow" (2 Corinthians 7:5–16). Almost anyone who has received a traffic ticket understands "worldly sorrow." Most of us regret being caught in some violation of the law. We dislike the inconvenience of going to court to pay a fine. We find ourselves embarrassed as we face the arresting officer. Perhaps we fear possible future consequences (e.g., higher car insurance rates).

All of us regret having our transgressions exposed—and not just in traffic court. In part, our regret comes from a fear of punishment. "Regret caused by fear" is one definition of "worldly sorrow." We, like our students, have experienced it often enough to recognize it instantly.

This worldly kind of sorrow can lead quickly into what the Scriptures sometimes call condemnation; a feeling of despair crashes in on us because we fear that we have out-sinned God's grace, have gone one step too far. Now, we fear, our Lord will impose upon us the penalties we rightly deserve for our sins; *this time* He will refuse to forgive us.

We might not put it in precisely these words. But we have all probably struggled with this feeling of condemnation from time to time. Christian teachers who listen carefully to their students will almost surely hear individual students who struggle with it too.

Worldly sorrow comes from Satan; it brings death. By way of contrast, Paul commends "godly sorrow." This kind of sorrow for sin leads us to the next step in God's process of repentance. Recognizing our sin and feeling its burden, we confess it.

The word for *confess* in the Greek of the New Testament means literally "to speak together" or "to say the same thing." When we confess our sins, we simply say what God says:

- We have indeed done what His Law has forbidden.

- Our action (thought, attitude) was wrong.

- Our sin hurt God; it hurt us; it hurt other people.

- We deserve God's punishment.

We come to God in honesty. We set aside our excuses. We forget about trying to shift the blame onto someone else's shoulders. We do not trivialize our sin. Nor do we minimize the penalties we deserve. We acknowledge with the apostle John, *"If we claim to be without sin, we deceive ourselves and the truth is not in us"* (1 John 1:8).

Standing then before God, stripped of all self-righteousness, we hear the beautiful words of our Father's absolution, *"If we confess our sins, He is faithful and just and will forgive us our sins and purify us from all unrighteousness"* (1 John 1:9).

Absolution is, for the Christian, a glorious emancipation proclamation. The Latin word from which we derive the English word *absolve* literally means "to set free; to release." Absolved from our sins, we find freedom from their guilt and shame. We thank God that we will not receive the punishment we have deserved.

And also—note this well—we receive in God's absolution *release from the power of our sins to enslave us.* That freedom comes, not as we try hard to amend our sinful lives, but as we rely on the Holy Spirit's power to "purify us from all unrighteousness." We realize that in our own strength, we cannot obey God. Left to our own resources, we do not even *want* to obey God. And so we ask Him to work these things in us. Note two of many New Testament passages that comment on this process:

> *It is God who works in you to will and to act according to His good purpose (Philippians 2:13).*

> *May the God of peace, who through the blood of the eternal covenant brought back from the dead our Lord Jesus, that great Shepherd of the sheep, **equip you with everything good for doing His will, and may He work in us what is pleasing to Him,** through Jesus Christ (Hebrews 13:20–21; emphasis added).*

Contrition. Confession. Absolution. Yielding to God's Spirit. We repeat this process of repentance often. We may, at times, find ourselves mired in a sin that we confessed only minutes before. In fact, we may find ourselves repeating the steps of the cycle a dozen times within a 10-minute period. But God will not become impatient or angry with us. He simply invites and encourages us to use the medicine He has prescribed. We can take it as often as we need it; we need not worry about overdosing.

As the Holy Spirit leads us through this process, He continually adds the surges of power we need so that, little by little, we can obey on ever-so-slightly higher a plane. By the Spirit's power, our cycle becomes a spiral headed gradually upward. Not that we will never fall back again into the same sins, but the general trend of our lives will be toward increasing Christ-likeness.

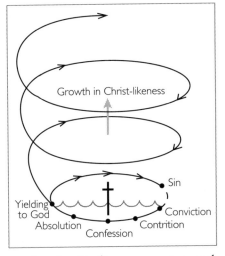

Most likely we will not see perceptible changes from day to day, but months or years into the future, we will look back and will worship God for what He has worked in our lives. We will see that we are becoming, by God's grace, more and more like Jesus. And we will know that all the credit for our growth belongs to Him:

> We, who with unveiled faces all reflect the Lord's glory, are being transformed into His likeness with ever-increasing glory, which comes from the Lord, who is the Spirit (2 Corinthians 3:18).

Perhaps all this seems too simple. Admittedly, it *is* simple, so simple that we could easily let our human pride prevent us from using it. It is simple—but it works. It is the only thing that works. And our Teacher yearns to help us use it so that we can live lives of fruitfulness, not frustration.

☧ FROM THE FILES

Case Study—"Aunty Nomian" versus "T. Ryan Hard"

Ms. Nomian has taught Sunday school for over two decades. In fact, she's become the mainstay, the backbone of the staff. The children and the other teachers alike love her; in fact, just about everyone calls her "Aunty."

Mr. Hard, the new Sunday school superintendent, knows all about Aunty. She was his first-grade teacher! He's thankful for her dedication, especially in light of how hard it is to recruit teachers. Still in some ways he feels a bit intimidated by her popularity. And he is determined to "shape up" the Sunday school.

In fact, the education committee chairperson who recruited Mr. Hard as superintendent has given him this task. Many of the long-time members of the congregation are appalled at the level of noise, laughter, and confusion that burst forth from the children's education wing of the building each Sunday.

Patrolling the hallway on his very first Sunday, Mr. Hard happened upon a conversation between Ms. Nomian and two of her first graders. It seems that Billy Sweatshirt had just popped Johnny Sweetly in the nose. Ms. Nomian was engaged in the process of trying to convince Johnny that he needed to forgive Billy (who stood smirking behind his lesson leaflet at the tear trickling down Johnny's cheek).

"No, no, no!" Mr. Hard exploded. "I'll handle this, Ms. Nomian! William, your last name ought to be Troublemaker. Well, you're not going to get away with it anymore. I'll see to that! You'll shape up and fly right from now on if you know what's good for you! Unless I see more effort on your part to behave yourself, I'm going to call your dad. Don't you know that Jesus doesn't love you when you act like this? You need to try harder to be good."

Ms. Nomian had been standing, staring at Mr. Hard with her mouth wide-open. Now she gasped aloud, grabbed Billy by the arm, yanked him back into the classroom, and slammed the door with a loud BANG.

"What got into her?" Mr. Hard asked Johnny, who at that moment burst into tears.

Think About This

Read through the case study, "Aunty Nomian Versus T. Ryan Hard" (p.42). Ask yourself, "What's wrong with this picture?" For example:

- From the standpoint of Law and Gospel, what's wrong with Ms. Nomian's idea that this situation can be resolved by somehow getting Johnny to forgive Billy?

- From the standpoint of Law and Gospel, what's wrong with Mr. Hard's idea that he can get Billy to "shape up" by somehow getting him to try harder?

- Suppose you're another teacher on the staff and you find Johnny sniffling in the bathroom after this whole incident. What would you say to him?

- Suppose you're a teacher on the staff and you overhear Billy telling all the other first-grade boys about what a crybaby Johnny is. What would you say to him?

- Suppose you were the chairperson of the education committee and you had just gotten a phone call from Mr. Hard, complaining about Ms. Nomian's lax discipline. How would you explain what the Bible says about God's process for making us more like Jesus? (*Write this out in your own words, and share it with another teacher or your pastor. What ideas, if any, do you still have trouble understanding or applying?*)

Do This

Intentionally practice the "Cycle of Repentance" in your own life today and during the next few weeks. Focus especially on the cross of your Savior and on the grace of God personalized to you at your Baptism. Notice the impact Law and Gospel make on your relationship with your Lord as you confess your sins.

[1] C. F. W. Walther, *Law and Gospel* (St. Louis: CPH, 1981. Walter Bouman, Tr.), pp. 32–33.

WHAT'S THE BIG IDEA?

CLASSROOM CLIMATE

4

Care to Change?

Think back to your own very first experience with the Christian faith—that is, the first significant experience you can remember. Use the space below to jot down as many details about that experience as you can. Include sights, sounds, smells. Think about what you were wearing. Think about who else was there with you. What happened? Who said what? What overall impressions did you have? Jot down as many details as you can. If you need more space, use another sheet of paper.

My First Significant Encounter with the Christian Faith

Now read what you've written. Does it primarily describe an early understanding of factual information about the faith? Or is it a memory about a relationship, an experience that shaped your early attitudes toward Jesus and His family, the church?

Perhaps you recall a quiet moment of peace in which Dad taught you your first bedtime prayer. Maybe you can still picture the smile on the face of your first Sunday school teacher welcoming you to class. Or maybe the encounter wasn't so pleasant—maybe you see yourself squirming in the pew, confined by hot, prickly "Sunday clothes" at a time when you wanted to be out running in the park.

Regardless of the details, when most people examine their early memories about the Christian faith, the memories they recall do not involve the specific words of the Ten Commandments or the biblical definition of justification or the details of our Lord's genealogy as recorded in Matthew 1. Most believers recall events connected by emotion, colored with relational content.

What does this tell us? Can we argue from this anecdotal evidence that those of us who teach in Christian classrooms should simply pitch the facts of the Christian faith overboard? That we should concentrate all our efforts at creating a "feel-good atmosphere" in which no one leaves without collecting a dozen "warm fuzzies"?

Not at all. Way back in chapter 1 as we looked at God's goals for His people's walk with Him, we established the importance of the facts of the faith. As we said then, God Himself has anchored Christianity in the bedrock of history. Christians who tear this anchor loose will find themselves drifting back and forth with every wave and wind of new doctrine that Satan can invent.

The exercise on the previous page does not illustrate a need to rid ourselves of faith's content. It does, though, underscore the truth that Christian teachers do need to pay attention to the other three dimensions of the Christian life we discussed back in chapter 1—faith, actions, and attitudes.

"McCHURCH"?

This chapter deals primarily with attitudes toward the things of God. How do attitudes develop? Can they be shaped? If so, how? Rather than examining a theoretical, academic perspective, let's look at a specific example of attitude formation, one quite familiar to most North Americans—the marketing strategies used by fast food restaurants.

Ask most any young person—from the toddler who can barely form a two-word sentence to the eighth grader planning his life's career—"Where would you like to go for lunch today?" Can you predict the response? A restaurant that promises to "treat you right"? One that will "do chicken right"? One that assures you that "you deserve a break today"?

You may be an adult "ready for some real food," and you may not even believe that fast food *is* real food. However, the students in the class you teach are likely to enjoy eating in fast food restaurants. Why?

Walk into any fast food franchise and look around through the eyes of a sociologist. Or better still, use the eyes of a four-, eight-, or twelve-year-old. What will you see?

- Chairs, tables, and maybe even a painting easel or a table of plastic building blocks designed for children

- Lots of light

- Cheerful colors

- Menu options that include meals packaged in boxes splashed with market-tested art and some intriguing toy trinket

- Music that appeals to the particular group of children or young people likely to be in the restaurant at that time of day

- Balloons, holiday decorations, videos, or posters that picture popular movie stars or sports heroes—each targeted to appeal to groups of youngsters of a specific age

Why do kids like these places? In short, kids know they belong there the minute they step onto the asphalt of the parking lot! The over-all "ambience"—the atmosphere—has been designed to say to children and teens, "We've planned for you. You're important to us. We've taken time to find out what you enjoy, and we want you to feel welcome here."

Note those verbs! *Designed. Planned. Taken time. Find out.* The climate in fast food restaurants didn't just happen. Someone thought it through. Someone planned for a specific effect—helping young customers feel welcome. Intentionality—it's key.

That's a key for Christian classrooms too. A warm, caring, cheerful, welcoming classroom atmosphere doesn't just happen by some kind of spiritual spontaneous combustion. Just "hoping to goodness" that our students feel welcome won't bring it about.

Over and over in the four gospels, we see Jesus welcoming children. In fact, throughout the Scripture we see our Lord taking care to include and welcome children in the family of faith.

BEYOND BALLOONS

Physical arrangements matter. The temperature and ventilation of the classroom count. Having enough space so students don't sit on top of each other is important. The fact that their teacher has prepared a bright, cheerful learning space means a lot to the learners who gather there. Even so, the quality of the teacher's relationship with the students will outshine the quality of the bulletin boards and the comfort of the chairs and tables every time.

What if Jesus had lived visibly on earth in our century and culture rather than in first-century Palestine. Would He have invented new recipes for pizza and handed out Happy Meals? I doubt it. However—and note this carefully, He most certainly would have aimed at the same goal as the fast food franchisers: welcoming children. His reasons for doing that would, of course, differ markedly from theirs. Nonetheless, we can be sure that He would have reached out to toddlers, teens, and every group in between.

With the idea of classroom climate in mind, read the familiar account of Jesus blessing the children. What did these children learn from their encounter with Christ?

> *They kept bringing young children to [Jesus] that He might touch them; and the disciples were reproving them [for it].*

But when Jesus saw [it], He was indignant and pained, and said to them, "Allow the children to come to Me—do not forbid or prevent or hinder them—for to such belongs the kingdom of God. Truly I tell you, whoever does not receive and accept and welcome the kingdom of God as a little child [does], positively shall not enter it at all."

And He took [the children up one by one] in His arms and (fervently invoked a) blessing, placing His hands upon them (Mark 10:13–16 AMP).

Jesus did not distribute helium balloons that day. Nor did He listen to anyone recite memory work. But who can doubt that these children went home more confident in the love and compassion of their Lord? Jesus touched their hearts by His words and in His actions to nurture and enrich their faith. His words and actions surely touched and warmed the attitude of their hearts with the fire of His concern for each of them individually. Faith and attitudes; these are critical components of any believer's relationship with our Savior.

Maybe you've heard the proverb: "People don't care how much you know until they know how much you care." That's especially true in Christian education. Our students need to know we care about them. They need to understand that our concern comes from Christ Jesus Himself; we serve them as His representatives. They need to experience that care in concrete ways, ways that make a difference in their lives. When that happens, they will listen with more interest to our words and to the facts we share about Jesus.

CARE TO CHANGE

Relationships are crucial in the disciple-making process. These relationships run vertically—between each individual student and the Lord Christ. And these relationships run horizontally—between each student and the other students, each student and the teacher.

Christ cares—deeply—about relationships in His church. He bled and died to bring each of us into His family. Recall how the apostle John, near the beginning of his new life of discipleship with Jesus, wanted to call fire down from heaven to destroy one of the villages of Samaria for not welcoming the Savior. Jesus nicked-

49

named John and his brother James "Sons of Thunder," perhaps because of this fierceness in the face of rejection.

Later this same apostle repeated one refrain again and again in the letters he wrote to his fellow believers late in his earthly life: "Love one another" (1 John 3:11; 3:23; 4:7; 4:11). Jesus changed John. He transformed him. We see evidence of this change in John's heart toward others.

Relationships matter in Christ's kingdom. They call for intentional attention in our classes. In fact, the Christian classroom is a perfect laboratory in which all of God's people can practice the love of which John wrote.

Quite often, teachers will attend to their own personal relationships with each of their students. These relationships *are* critical from a disciple-making point of view. But we also need to pay attention to the relationships of our students with one another. I personally know more than one family that has dropped out of congregational worship life because of the way their children were treated by other children in the Sunday school. How sad! Really, how demonic!

Satan works and schemes to demolish relationships in the body of Christ. Because this is true, we need to pray and work toward thwarting his strategies. Prayer counts. God responds to our prayers. He helps us understand what to do to prevent problems in the first place. He shows us where to get help with our specific problems when they do arise.

PRACTICALLY PROACTIVE

The list that follows contains big things and little things you can do. These practices may brighten the climate in your classroom and foster relationships of concern and care between and among your students and yourself. No one can add all of these suggestions into his or her classroom practices at once. Some of the ideas will work best in early childhood classrooms; others will fit more appropriately into a junior high routine.

Start small. Choose one or two ideas to try at first. Keep those that work for you. Discard those that don't. Is it worth the extra time and trouble? Yes. A fresh and inviting classroom atmosphere often leads to fewer discipline problems. As a result, you may enjoy teaching more. And more your students may want to spend time in your classroom, learning to know, love, and become like their Savior.

- Take a page out of the fast food menu. Do what you can to make your classroom bright and colorful. Certainly be sure it is clean, well-ventilated, and at a comfortable temperature.

- Identify ways to give the students a sense of ownership in "their room." Display their art. Involve them in choosing posters for the walls. Let them make banners or mobiles to hang from the ceiling. Place all visuals at the students' eye-level.

- If you share a learning space with other groups that meet at other times, find ways to compromise with them about displays from your class. Or find easy ways to put up and take down your decorations each time you meet. Let your students help you do this.

- Be in your area when the students arrive. Smile as you greet them. If you teach younger children, squat or stoop to meet them at their eye-level, not as a tall (and perhaps frightening) adult.

- Be prepared! Come to class ready to teach. Use the time before the class period begins to chat with your students.

- Plan a variety of age-appropriate activities for each class period, and keep things moving along. Repeat kinds of activities that motivate and challenge your students. Eliminate methods that fall flat.

- Have everything you need on hand as you begin. This practice, all by itself, will eliminate many discipline problems.

- Plan more activities than you will need. It's better to walk in overprepared and have to choose among several possible activities as you go along than to run out of productive things to do.

- Notice and comment on the little things—the new hair cut, the happy smile. Celebrate the big things—a birthday, a new baby brother. Ask about the important things—last week's math test, Grandma's hospitalization.

- Play Christian music softly as the class arrives. Often this technique will keep the classroom noise level down while enhancing a feeling of cheerfulness and of the Lord's presence. (Choose songs with lyrics that reinforce the biblical truths you want to teach. Avoid songs that reinforce moralism. See chapter 3 for a fuller discussion.)

- Catch individuals being good and affirm them for it. Better still, catch them being good and report it to Mom and Dad!

- Affirm. Affirm. Affirm. Affirm not just for things that individuals *do,* but for who they *are* as Jesus' people. Make frequent statements like these: "I'm so glad you've come today"; "Wow, I'm happy Jesus has put us together in this class"; "I appreciate your thoughtful answer"; "Look how well Erin followed directions"; "What an insightful question!"

- Talk about the power of affirmation and of encouraging one another. Study texts such as 1 Thessalonians 4:18; 5:11; 2 Thessalonians 2:17; Hebrews 3:13; and Hebrews 10:25 with older students as together you brainstorm ways to make your classroom a place where affirmation and encouragement happen more and more often.

- Structure each classroom situation for success and reward it. Help students spot and feel good about the Christ-likeness the Holy Spirit is building into their lives.

- Work toward cooperation in learning. Let the students work together toward a common goal—packing food for hungry neighbors, praying for secret prayer partners, analyzing the hidden messages in ads, completing a Bible study activity.

Think About This

"People don't care how much you know until they know how much you care." In what kinds of situations is this statement not necessarily true? In what kinds of situations is it not only true, but of critical importance?

Picture your students in your mind's eye. Make a list in the space below. Identify five ways you could demonstrate your care for each of them in the next few weeks. Use these three criteria:

- Your ideas must be simple and must take no longer than a few minutes to carry out.

- Your ideas must be free or very inexpensive.

- Your ideas must be things you are willing to do and would enjoy doing.

Do This

Walk into your classroom as if you were seeing it for the first time. If you teach younger children, get down on your knees so you can look around from the children's eye-level.

- What one thing could you do *right now* to make the space more appealing for the learners who spend time here each time your class meets? Do it.

- What changes would you like to make, but can't right now for some reason? To whom could you talk about those changes? What compromise or trade-off might you be willing to make with that person? Pick up the phone or make an appointment.

- Suppose you had an extra $10 and wanted to spend it on something to brighten up your learning space. What would you get? Often, little things can make a big difference. Pray about it, and then ask the person in charge of your program for permission to get it. Be prepared to explain exactly what difference it will make and why that difference is important.

WHAT'S THE BIG IDEA?

APPROPRIATE PRACTICES

5

Teaching for a Change in Kids

Here we stand, at the beginning of chapter 5. Maybe you find yourself a bit surprised that it has taken this long to get to a discussion of the class session itself—the lesson plan and what teachers do so learning happens. This was no oversight. It is a deliberate attempt to drive home the importance of those things that might seem peripheral to learning.

You see, everything we've discussed so far counts. Adequate lighting. Your personal prayer life. The ways you understand and apply Law and Gospel in your own walk with Jesus. The compliment you pay to the child with new shoes. The moments you spend chatting with the student you chance to meet in the aisle at the supermarket. None of this is inconsequential. None is mere window dressing.

Teachers like to assume that the lessons we teach are what our students learn. After all, that's why we go back to our class week after week. That's why we plan with so much care. We expect to make a difference. We expect our students will learn what we teach. Isn't our lesson the main thing?

Maybe. Or maybe not. Perhaps you know the little proverb, "Life is what happens while you're waiting around for something else." We might crop that proverb to fit the classroom in words like this: "Education is what happens to students while they're waiting around for class to start."

In our more pessimistic moments (and even teachers in Christian classrooms have them), we may despair of our students ever learning anything. Not so! They are learning all the time. Suppose, for instance, they walk into a cheerful, orderly classroom with lots of interesting activities already going on. What might they learn?

- The setting tells them that their teacher cares enough about them to spend time preparing for their visit in God's house. They will likely feel welcome and important.

- They will likely conclude that since God's people welcome children so readily, the Lord Himself must do that too.

- They will learn to look forward to coming to God's house to enjoy the security of being in Jesus' presence.

- They will realize that learning about the Lord is an important, exciting, challenging, life-changing thing to do.

On the other hand, if the classroom is chaotic, hot, and drab, and their teacher has not yet arrived, they will learn something else.

During recent decades educators have talked about a concept some have called "the hidden curriculum." This "hidden curriculum" includes the lessons students learn from

- the bully in the bathroom;

- their friendships on the playground;

- the expressions on their teacher's face;

- the methods of discipline practiced by the adults in the school;

- their experiences in coping with the bus ride home;

In short, the "hidden curriculum" involves the education no one plans. It includes events and relationships teachers might not ever even think about. It includes many things we may want to ignore, telling ourselves they really don't matter that much.

We may wish otherwise, but the hidden curriculum packs a big wallop! Someone has estimated that as much as 80–90% of what students learn in school comes from the "hidden curriculum." Educators say this is true for schools where the facts of math and reading take a front row seat. How could it be less true for Christian classrooms in which facts matter, but where faith, attitudes, and behaviors combine with facts to form the core of what we intend to teach?

We cannot let ourselves be fooled into thinking that nothing counts except the lesson we plan. We may even want to reconsider the notion that the lesson we plan counts most. Especially in the church, education may be what happens to students while they wait for class to begin and the "peripherals" that exist while we carry out our plan.

Does all this mean that you can forget about planning and simply decide to let what happens in class happen? Of course not. In fact, the rest of this chapter will guide you through an in-depth process of lesson planning.

Still, we dare not miss the point that "peripherals" aren't necessary peripheral. Particularly, our relationships with students influence their picture of Jesus and their relationship with Him. And that's what matters most. That's an eternal possession. That's the main thing. As we teach, we need to "keep the main thing the main thing."

TEACHER, WHERE ARE WE GOING?

Have you ever gone camping with a group of scouts? Or joined forces with other families to caravan down the highway on vacation together? Or gone biking or canoeing or even white water rafting with a group of your friends? If so, you've experienced something of the sense of high adventure that goes along with traveling with others through a set of common challenges toward a common goal.

In many ways, teaching the faith is like that. You already know our ultimate goal—transformation into the full image of Christ (pp. 9–16). You already know how that transformation happens—as God's people, by God's grace, access His power through Word and Sacrament and grow in discipleship.

All of us in God's family are people in process, people on a journey, people headed toward a common destiny. And as we walk step-by-step along the way, we cheer one another on. We encourage one another. We teach one another. And sometimes we challenge and even confront one another.

Like people on a journey together, we set aside times to talk to one another about where we've been and where we're headed. We share our exhilaration and our blisters. And we stake out goals for the day or week ahead. When we take time to think through what God has done and where we want to go—not just ultimately, but also the intermediate stops in between—we're much more likely to arrive. We're also more likely to appreciate the scenery along the way and to have the motivation we need to climb the hills that pop up along the route.

Think of the time you spend with your students in that way for a moment. Think of your time together in class as a rest-break along the trail. Think of it as a time to refresh yourselves with the cool water of God's Word and to take out the map to see just where you might be headed next.

As the teacher—the discipler, the more mature believer in the group—you have the authority from God and from your congregation to decide how best to use the group's time. With that authority comes responsibility—the responsibility to set goals and to design a plan to meet those goals.

Goals. Objectives. Desired outcomes. Whatever you call them, they express in a concise way the destination at which you want the group to arrive when the year, the month, the week, or the hour ends.

Of course, we have no power in and of ourselves to bring our vision of Christ-likeness for ourselves and for our students into reality. The Spirit of God must do His holy work, both in our own hearts and in the hearts of our students. Nevertheless, God has promised to use His Word—the Word spoken by His people—to accomplish His purposes (Isaiah 55:10–11). Relying on His promise, we set goals for each class session—transformational goals! Goals that will mean real differences in the lives of our students!

In chapter 1, we studied verses from Psalm 78 in detail. There we saw four dynamics that form the core of our Lord's goals for the lives of His people: Faith. Facts. Attitudes. Actions. The Scriptures address these dynamics so consistently that we cannot miss the point: If the Holy Spirit were to write Christian curriculum, He would focus on them. These dynamics have, in fact, been the focus of His work in the lives of His people from Old Testament times onward.

As you plan the goals for each lesson you teach, you need to keep each of these dynamics in mind too. Does that mean you will always have four goals? Probably not. Will each of the four dynamics of the believer's relationship with the Lord appear in each lesson's goal statements? Yes, although from session to session you will accent each to varying degrees. You may, for example, weight one lesson more heavily toward factual knowledge, while the next lesson contains perhaps no new facts whatsoever but focuses instead on a specific attitude or behavior.

Where do goals come from? The most powerful goals converge from two different directions—the truths of Holy Scripture and the needs of individual learners. Our need. God's provision. When the power of God's Word touches the needs of God's children, teachers can stand back and watch God do His transforming work in the hearts of His people.

That point of intersection is where love—true, Christ-like love—blossoms. Hope is born. Confidence in God's promises ignites and glows brighter and brighter. The deep kind of peace that makes the world shake its head in wonder takes root. Transformation occurs as human need meets God's provision.

Truth be told, my first few years of teaching involved very little goal setting of the kind I just described. I usually read the list of "Desired Outcomes" from the teachers guide I used at the time. But for the most part, I knew I would "teach Noah's Ark." So what did the specifics matter? I could just lead my class through the Bible story and trust God to use it in the lives of my students.

Or so I thought. Then, slowly but surely, I found myself more and more dissatisfied with what went on in class. The students seemed to like me. Their words and actions said they enjoyed coming to class. They even learned the facts about Noah's ark. But I saw little spiritual growth. Sometimes I thought I might as well have been teaching Aesop's fables.

With this discouragement came the Holy Spirit's conviction. I had learned enough during my four years in teachers college about helping students grow in their discipleship. But once I graduated and had a class of my own, I had been unwilling to take the time and expend the effort to discern the points at which the Scriptures intersected my students' joys, hurts, sins, and hopes. I aimed at nothing in particular. And I hit it!

Older and wiser, I now pay close attention to the task of writing lesson goals. Sometimes, this takes more time than any other part of the planning process. First, I pray and wrestle with the text *for myself:*

- What does it say?

- What does it mean?

- What does it mean for *me?*

Until I have allowed the Holy Spirit to put His finger on the "sore spots" of sin and guilt, fear and spiritual immaturity in my own heart, until I have confessed my own sins and looked into Jesus' eyes for the assurance of His forgiveness and hope for my own life, how can I presume to lead others through that process?

Then I pray and wrestle with the text for my students:

- How will they understand what it says?

- How can I best communicate with it means?

- What does the text mean—for each of them *personally?* And how can they best be led to see that?

Won't a planning process like that take lots of time? Yes. Doesn't it imply that we know the learners very well? Yes again. But if we intend, by the Holy Spirit's power, truly to *disciple* those who enter our classroom week after week, we need to be willing to expend the effort required.

But (dare we think it?) what if some weeks we're *not* willing? When that's the case (and it will be for all of us from time to time), we need to take that attitude to the cross, just as we take all our other sins there. We need to confess it; we need to receive from our Savior His forgiveness; and we need to ask for His motivation and power—and yes, for the joy—we need to lead the learners He has so graciously entrusted to us.

One final note on goal-setting. Research consistently shows that learners achieve lesson goals best when they know what the goals are as the class session begins. When everyone in the classroom starts out knowing where they're headed, they all are much more likely to arrive at that point when class ends! We need not keep our goals a secret. Nor should we. But we do need to explain them in terms our students can understand.

TOP

Stop for a moment here. Think about these questions and jot down some of your thoughts before you go on.

1. *Look over a lesson plan you taught recently, target the objectives/goals in particular—either those that appear in your teachers guide or those you modified for your specific group of students. Where do these goals address faith?*

   facts?

   attitudes?

   actions?

2. *Can all of our goals in Christian education be observed or measured? Explain.*

3. *What advantages do observable, measurable goals have?*

4. *How can you tell from Jesus' interaction with His disciples that He knew them well and that He had specific goals in mind for their walk with Him? (Give two or more examples.)*

TEACHER, HELP ME KNOW GOD'S LOVE

Once you have a destination in mind, you need to pick an appropriate vehicle for getting there. You can't get from San Francisco to Tokyo by hiking, no matter how sincere your intentions. In the same way, some classroom activities will take you toward one goal, other activities will take you toward another goal. One of the most exciting challenges of Christian education involves choosing from among many methods to achieve specific lesson goals.

Good lessons start where the learners are and lead them toward Christ's goals for their lives. In other words, good lessons show progression. They don't just wander from one activity to another. One step leads to the next.

Look back at the diagram of the cycle of repentance (p. 38). If we believe that this represents the process the Holy Spirit uses to bring about change, to bring about spiritual growth in the lives of His people, then arguably each lesson we plan needs to involve the students in working through this cycle. They need to identify the sin in their lives, admit that it's there, realize the hurt it causes them and those around them, confess that sin to their Savior, and receive His forgiveness and His power—His transformational power.

Does this sound dreary or bleak or monotonous—all this talk about sin and grace, Law and Gospel, the process of repentance and forgiveness? It need not be! In fact, teaching and learning to live this kind of lifestyle, a Christian lifestyle, can become one of life's most riveting adventures.

Does this mean that every lesson must include a formal confession of sins and declaration of forgiveness? No. Does it mean every lesson will sound alike? Of course not. Does it mean no one can have fun in Sunday school or Confirmation class? Absolutely not! When we see how the crowds swarmed around Jesus as He taught during the years of His earthly ministry, we can hardly deduce that He used a sour, crotchety approach to discipling His listeners.

It *does* mean, though, that we let nothing deter us from plugging into the only true power source we have: the Gospel!

Think of it! Our sins can never again threaten to drown us in the sea of guilt. Satan can no longer dangle the sword of God's anger over our heads. We need never again listen when the devil tries to lie to us about our true identity. The shame we may feel because of things we have done or failed to do cannot turn us into losers. The victory and power that Jesus died to win for us gives us a whole new potential—all the potential that goes with our new life as children of the Lord Most High. Life has higher purposes than human beings could ever have dreamed possible. What's more, this life here and now is only the foyer to the mansion of forever where we will live eternally with one another and with the Lord Jesus!

That's our message, the message of Law and Gospel, sin and grace. What a shame—really, what a sin—to bore those who come to learn more about that message from us! What a shame—really, what a sin—to downplay that message or to set it aside for any reason! We have something real. Something that makes life work.

Something that gives life meaning. How can we most effectively communicate it?

TEACHER, IS THIS FUN?

Nowhere does our culture threaten to suck the church of Jesus Christ under with such violent force as in the river of Christian education. On the one hand, we see teachers who "teach as they were taught." These volunteers mean well. But they often fail to become catalysts of Christ-like growth in their students' lives.

Why? Many students today do not learn well when subjected to the educational methods of previous generations. The world around them has changed. Their experiences have changed. Their expectations have changed. Younger and younger students resist the former methods of Christian education. They register their verdict by voting with their feet; they simply just don't return to classes run like these. Fewer and fewer parents will argue with a son or daughter who makes that decision.

On the other end of the spectrum, we find Christian education packaged as "edutainment"—an amalgam composed supposedly of equal parts entertainment and education. If you want to be tried for heresy in some churches today, forget about denying the doctrine of the Trinity or tinkering around with the deity and humanity of Christ. Instead, try suggesting that the great North American idol, Fun, has become our most popular false god—and that many of his worshipers regularly bow to him in the Christian education wing of the church building!

Small towns. Inner cities. Suburbs. Rural areas of North America. Instant access to all kinds of information and the ease of travel have erased most of the cultural differences that may once have separated them. Sad to say, this erasure did not give downtown Los Angeles, Chicago, Detroit, Dallas, or Baltimore the proverbial peace and relative safety of the small town. Rather, the villages that dot our countryside have imported the culture of the cities.

No matter where we live, we watch as our children drown in a rising tide of violence, materialism, loneliness, and the moral morass of relativism. We may rage against this. We may panic in the face of it. Or we may simply want to give up. Still the question haunts us (or it should)—what are we as God's people, as teachers in God's church, doing to help these kids live the "abundant life" our Lord Jesus promised His people they could and would live—the life He made it possible for us to live?

How can we "teach for a change" in a culture like ours? Games of Bible baseball won't do it—if, indeed, they ever did. Bible trivia in whatever form (no matter how "fun") won't do it. Coloring book pictures used as kindergarten crowd control won't do it. Mindless fill-in-the-blank exercises won't do it. Teachers who stand on their heads and spit nickels to keep their classes happy and returning won't do it either.

To "teach for a change" we must design and implement classroom activities that will:

- direct students to Christ, their crucified and risen Savior and friend;

- involve the students in identifying their own specific needs for the Lord's help;

- help the students identify places where God's Word, His power and His promises intersect their needs;

- lead the students in confessing specific sins;

- show the students how to draw on God's power to change, and provide activities that give them the opportunity to do just that;

- encourage the learners to respond to God's goodness in specific acts of worship and thanksgiving;

- make Christian community come alive for all learners and teachers so that everyone in the classroom can "Encourage one another and build each other up" (1 Thessalonians 5:11), and so that in times of stress and temptation they can know the comfort and support of the holy Christian church, the communion of saints.

APPROPRIATE PRACTICES

In one sense, spiritual growth will always mystify human beings, because God must work it in His people from beginning to end. We cannot transform ourselves or anyone else.

In another sense, though, we know quite a lot about the kinds of activities that best nurture spiritual growth. We plan and use these "appropriate practices." With God's power our personal foibles and idiosyncrasies fade more and more into the background, and the Holy Spirit has more and more opportunity to work through His Word in the hearts of our students. Appropriate practices for Christian education grow, at least in part, out of what we know in general about how people—children and adults alike—learn.

We know, for instance, that:

- people learn best when—from the beginning of the lesson—they see the value for their lives of the material to be learned;

- people learn best when the lesson begins with some kind of activity to engage them—to help them make a smooth transition from their everyday lives into the lesson material;

- people learn best when learning activities are hands-on; not just theoretical or "heady";

- people learn best when the learning task engages all five senses or as many of these as practical (e.g., seeing, hearing, and tasting is usually more effective than simply listening);

- people learn best when they interact with others, evaluating ideas, discussing observations, exploring new truths, and thinking through the implications of those truths;

- most children and many adults learn best when the lesson deals with concrete ideas (e.g., object lessons designed around the truth that "Jesus is the Light," however clever or dramatic, will make no sense to most five- or 10-year-olds);

- people learn best when they receive frequent rewards affirming their ability to learn and their progress toward specific goals;

- people learn best in a safe, comfortable learning environment, one in which distractions are kept to a minimum and in which they feel comfortable with the teacher/leader and with the other learners in the group;

- "the mind can only absorb what the posterior can withstand"—even adult learners learn best when they can change position every 30 minutes or so; in general, the younger the learners, the more often they need to move around and the more frequently the teacher needs to move from one activity into the next;

- different people learn differently; for maximum learning, teachers need to include a variety of learning activities in any given lesson plan;

- learners tend to "do as we do" no matter how much we wish they would "do as we say"; Christian teachers who want to disciple their students need to model in their own lives the attitudes and actions they want to see in the lives of their students;

- people retain what they learn when it is meaningful to them, when they can put it to use in their lives right away, and when it is repeated in different ways over a period of weeks, months, or even years.

ARE WE THERE YET?

Those words are *the* vacation joke in most families. Someone may ask the question before the car leaves the driveway, and if not then, at least before you've covered 10 blocks.

Christian teachers do well to ask it of themselves too as they move through a lesson and certainly as each day's lesson ends. Now, of course, we're talking about evaluation. Most times those who teach in a congregation's part-time agencies will not use formal tests or homework assignments. So how will we know when we're "there"?

A friend of mine teaches a group of adults with developmental disabilities. At one time one of her students who, while in class nearly every Sunday, could not speak. The young lady's parents wanted her to be baptized, and one morning the pastor came to the classroom to talk to the student about that. His first question was simple, "Do you love Jesus?"

A smile beamed from the student's face. She leaped up from her chair, ran to the classroom altar, picked up the cross—and hugged it.

That "evaluation activity," simple and informal though it was, told more about the relationship between the Lord and His precious child than a 500 question multiple-choice exam ever could.

We may sometimes use a test or ask the class to write out the memory verse we assigned for the day. Most times, though, our evaluation will remain more informal. As the lesson ends each day, for example, we will review the day's goals or objectives. As we do, we might ask ourselves:

- What evidence did I see or hear of the students' growing trust in Jesus—for time and for eternity?

- What facts still seem fuzzy? to which students?

- Did the Holy Spirit convict us of our sins? How do I know that?

- With what words and actions did the students and I assure one another of God's full and free forgiveness?

- How have we asked the Holy Spirit to change our attitudes and our actions? Did we practice these changes in any specific way? With what results?

- What worked well? What activities would I like to use again? What didn't go so well? Could I improve my approach in some way or would it be best to eliminate that kind of activity in future planning?

After you have used questions like these to think your way through the class session, pray. Ask the Lord to use His Word, just as He has promised, to continue to work His transformation in the hearts and lives of both you and your students. Ask Him to deepen your own discipleship and sharpen your skills for discipling others. Thank Him for what went well. Then ask for His help with your next lesson plan.

Think About This

Think about the "hidden curriculum" your students may encounter in connection with their experience in your classroom.
  a. What good things may form part of the "hidden curriculum" of my students?
  b. What one part of that "hidden curriculum" would I like to work to change this week? How could I go about that? Who could help me or support me in it?

Try This

As you prepare the next lesson you will teach, read the Bible text. Then think about where the text intersects the needs and hurts of your students.
  1. Write four objectives based on the text and the students' needs, one for each of the four dynamics of Christian growth —faith, facts, attitudes, actions.

    • Was this exercise easy or hard? Explain.

    • How did writing your own goals change the way you planned? the way you taught? your attitude toward the "disciples" whom you taught?

  2. Look back over your lesson plan.

    • Where is the Law?

    • Where is the Gospel?

    • Which part(s) of the lesson answer your students' question, "Now that I know this, what do I do?"

Age 4

1. Views prayer as "talking to God"
2. Recognizes the Bible as "God's Book"
3. Distinguishes make-believe from reality and associates Bible stories with reality
4. Exhibits a simple, deep faith in Jesus

Age 5

1. Visualizes Jesus as a person
2. Recognizes the Bible as a special book that tells us how God wants people to live
3. Enjoys "church" activities (singing, learning, praying)
4. Feels secure in God's love and care
5. Thinks in literal, factual, and concrete terms
6. Enjoys repetition and humor

Ages 6 and 7

1. Have a vague understanding of God because they do not think in abstract terms
2. Can understand that God is our heavenly Father; that God gives us everything; that Jesus is God's son; that Jesus died on the cross for each one of us
3. Feel they do no wrong and thus lack true repentance
4. See only the wrongs of others
5. Find unconditional love hard to accept
6. Show complete trust in their heavenly Father
7. Consider actions as wrong only if caught or punished
8. Apply the letter of the Law rather than the spirit of the law
9. Favor severe punishment to "pay back" for the wrong
10. Show curiosity about death, dying, and heaven

Ages 8 and 9

1. Have internalized their concept of God and can share their faith quite readily
2. Are able to study the Bible chronologically
3. Enjoy learning about heroes of the Bible
4. Are better able to understand the church's role in world missions
5. See God at work in the every day world
6. Are generally able to tell someone who has hurt them their wrong rather than tattling to the teacher
7. Pray readily for others
8. Continue to derive satisfaction from helping others
9. Are growing in ability to carry on deep discussions about God and their Christian fatih
10. Are building moral standards that will help them make difficult decisions

Ages 10 and 11

1. Are capable of deep religious feeling
2. Seek a powerful influence in their lives (look for models, heroes)
3. Have a questioning nature in religious matters
4. Have developed a conscience
5. See God as more rational and less vindictive than earlier
6. See Jesus as God's Son, but don't really know what this means
7. See goodness and badness in everyone, but see it quantitatively
8. Accept the Bible as true because God gives it authority
9. Expect immediate answers to prayer
10. Pray in a less egocentric and materialistic way than primary children

Ages 12 and 13

1. Are able to understand concepts of increased complexity
2. Contemplate the mysteries of the Christian faith
3. Wonder about and try to resolve questions about attributes of God, concept of the Trinity, the virgin birth
4. Marvel at the awesomeness of the creation of which they are a part and wonder within themselves what the Maker's special plan is for them
5. Are able to see the hand of God at work in history and in the world around them
6. Can understand the redemptive work of Jesus Christ more fully and also can appreciate it in a deeper and more personal way

Adapted from *Teachers Interaction*, copyright © 1990 Concordia Publishing House.

WHAT'S THE BIG IDEA?

■

WINDOWS OF OPPORTUNITY

6

Challenges to Change

The class had sung the opening hymn and Angela had begun to read a Bible verse. She got as far as the third word when the classroom door swung open with a loud THUD. Spike waltzed through the doorway, tripped on his shoe lace, and fell flat on his face in the middle of the aisle. He looked up at me, grinned, and then giggled, "I'm here!"

Later, in the quiet of the corridor, after the class had begun working on the first lesson activity, I looked into Spike's eyes and sighed. This was not the first time we had stood in the corridor together. Nor, I knew, would it be the last. Half-rhetorically, I asked, "What am I going to do with you, Spike?"

Spike sighed too. Then he answered in a matter-of-fact tone, "I don't know, Miss Fryar. You could spank me. You haven't tried that yet. But my mom does it all the time, and it never seems to help."

As I look on the rest of the "little chat" Spike and I had that day, I feel even less happy about it than I did then. Knowing what I know now about Law and Gospel, knowing and believing what I've learned since about discipling (note: not "disciplining") kids, I'm not proud of where Spike and I ended our conversation.

I like to think that when the next "Spike" and I meet up, I will better represent the Lord Jesus. I pray that I will be better equipped to lead Spike through the process of repentance. I pray that he will see more fruit and will experience less frustration in his walk with the Lord Jesus—at church and at home—as a result of the time he will spend in my class. I thank our Lord that He forgives even the sins we commit as teachers in His church, and that He makes the "next times" possible for us, despite those failures.

We begin this chapter on how to deal with sin in the Christian classroom by admitting to ourselves and to one another that no one handles situations like Spike's late (and dramatic) arrival perfectly all the time. In fact, the notion that there is a perfect way to handle any discipline problem can create unnecessary regret and second-guessing.

ACT—SO YOU NEED NOT REACT!

We also begin by reminding ourselves that all teachers at times find themselves facing misbehavior—by individuals or by the whole class. The last perfect Child to walk around on this earth grew up to become the last perfect Teacher to walk around on this earth—about 2000 years ago. So whether you are a professional teacher or a volunteer, you will likely find yourself concerned about misbehavior from time to time—or even from minute to minute.

As we have seen in previous chapters, a proactive approach to classroom management can help teachers accomplish their goals. This approach can also prevent many behavior problems. For the sake of learning as well as good order:

- Be on hand, ready to greet the students as they arrive.

- Pay attention to relationships. Ask yourself, "Do the students know my name? the names of their classmates? What have we done together that will help everyone realize they are an important part of this "team," partners in the Gospel doing things together for Jesus and for others (Philippians 1:3–5)?

- Make sure learning begins when the first student arrives. Have engaging, productive activities related to the lesson out and ready to go.

- Affirm. Affirm. Affirm. Don't let positive behavior go unnoticed. Help every student in your group, no matter how old or young, remember who they are—the King's Kids, precious to the Lord. Remind them often that Jesus lives and works within them and is writing their life-story as a unique poem of joy and praise (see Ephesians 2:10).

- Keep rules to a minimum. Make sure everyone understands them. Whether or not you involve the students in developing classroom rules is really a matter of personal teaching style. Regardless, keep the rule list simple and positive. (For example, In this class, we help and respect each other; we listen to each other; we ask for help when we need it; we admit our wrongs and ask God and each other for forgiveness.)

- Admit your own sins and ask those whom you have hurt to forgive you. Model confession. Remember, we all stand on level ground with our students beneath the cross. Sometimes teachers fear that admitting their own need for Jesus' pardon will diminish their students' respect for them. Rather, it usually will strengthen the authority of your words as you speak the Gospel.

- Teach the Cycle of Repentance (p. 38) to your group before a crisis arises. (Even young children can learn its dynamics in a simplified form.) Help them understand what it means in your own life. Then, when you need to walk a student or group through it, they will already have the "head-knowledge" they need to let the Lord Jesus use His Law and His Gospel to touch and transform their hearts.

WASP ATTACK!

The first day of school. My 34 fourth graders sat straight in their desks as I distributed textbooks and listened to stories about the events of the summer now past. A breeze blew through the windows that lined the entire east wall of the classroom. The windows had no screens; the harsh cold of Milwaukee winters kept insect problems to a minimum.

I'm sure the hapless wasp that flew into the fourth grade classroom that morning had no idea what he had gotten himself into. Mark spied him first. He leaped from his chair, a rolled up reading workbook clenched in his fist. "I'll get him, Miss Fryar," he shouted. Startled, I looked up. Just then, two girls saw the wasp. Simultaneously, they each let out an "Oooooooooo," lurched out from behind their desks, and (inexplicably) bounded up to stand on their chairs.

"I'll get him, Miss Fryar!" Mark shouted again. Five other boys rolled up their reading workbooks and followed Mark down the aisle. All the girls in the room let out a second, "Oooooooo."

Just as pandemonium took over, the classroom door opened. In walked the principal with a mother and a new student. "I'll get him!" roared Mark again. "A wasp," I explained, red-faced, to the two adults who stood in the doorway, eyebrows raised.

That wasp attack ranks as one of my top-five most embarrassing moments. Even now, even as I grin at the memory, I feel somewhat abashed. Still, I realize that had the Angel Gabriel been in charge of that particular class that day and had that wasp flown in the window, the children would have reacted in much the same way.

Setting unrealistic expectations for students' behavior can make dealing with some situations more difficult—or even impossible. So can personalizing student behaviors. Mark and his classmates acted like most fourth graders will when wasps fly in the open window of their classroom. I knew that. Even so, at the time, I saw the incident somehow as a reflection on me and on my effectiveness as a teacher—especially since I felt somewhat insecure as a new teacher in a new school with a new class and a new principal and parent watching.

When particular student behaviors cause us problems, we need some kind of filter to help us "choose our battles." At least from my perspective and experience, some behaviors, though bothersome, are best ignored. Other behaviors, even misbehaviors that seem unimportant, need immediate attention. How can we tell the difference? When student behaviors cause us distress, we can ask ourselves questions like these. Such questions that will help us distinguish between situations like Spike's, on the one hand, and Mark's on the other.

- Do my students know my expectations? Do they understand them?

- Are my expectations reasonable for the developmental level of my students and for this particular situation? In other words, is this simply normal childhood curiosity, exuberance, etc., or is it misbehavior?

- Since behavior that is ignored will often disappear, can I ignore it right now? Or is it sin that I, as God's representative, need to confront immediately?

- Have I contributed to the problem in any way (e.g., by not arriving on time, preparing inadequately, embarrassing a student in front of his/her peers)?

- What am I praying for this group of students and for the individuals in it? How might I better focus my prayers? How can more of God's power and blessing flow through my time with this class?

WHAT DID YOU EXPECT?

Children simply are not "miniature adults." Children think differently than we as adults do. They base their decisions on different ways of looking at the world. They reason differently than adults. (See the charts on pp. 71–73.)

Children's growing bodies (and for adolescents, changing hormones) and their zest for exploration and learning challenge us. At times it seems impossible for them to sit wiggleless and quiet while they listen to someone talk at them.

Does all of this mean that we excuse disruptive behavior? Or that we tolerate behaviors by one student or a small group of students who keep the whole class from learning? Of course not. It does mean, though, that we learn to adjust our expectations to fit both our students' developmental abilities and the situation. It also means that we distinguish between a simple wasp attack and World War III.

For instance, preschool children may be able to sit and listen to their teacher tell a Bible story for two or three minutes. If she has pictures they can look at as they hear the story, their attention span might stretch an additional minute or two. On the other hand, when they are actively engaged, at the play dough table, for instance, they may be able to sit for 20 minutes.

The morning after a classmate's dad dies, a fourth grade class may sit for an hour simply listening as you answer their questions about death, about heaven, about the resurrection, and about Jesus' second coming. They may gobble up whole pages from the book of Revelation. They may eagerly memorize parts of 1 Corinthians 15. On the other hand, a lesson on those same topics may fall as flat as yesterday's soda pop the morning on which the season's first snow flakes drift down outside the classroom windows.

We need to ask ourselves, "What's reasonable with this group of students in this particular situation?" If we expect too little, we will jeopardize our students' learning. If we expect too much, we set ourselves and our students up to fail.

As we think about setting reasonable expectations, we take into account both the dynamics of the group and situations in the individual lives of our students. A friend of mine who teaches preschool tells about one child who just could not sit still one morning. She disrupted the entire group for almost an hour. Finally, one of the helpers took her out to the playground where she slid down the slide (by actual count) a total of 37 times. When she returned to class, she listened and played calmly the rest of the class day.

Every student who enters your class carries an invisible knapsack. Some students come with theirs stuffed full of worries, family arguments, put-downs, fears, and pain. Many come with lighter loads—the goal they scored in last night's game, the B they got on Friday's math test, the pet rabbit Mom gave them for their birthday last week.

Sometimes a lesson plan with a strong opening activity will help each individual make the transition from life outside the classroom to the Scriptural truths you want to help them learn and build into their lives. But sometimes individuals have trouble taking off their knapsack. Sometimes it's too heavy. Sitting with a knapsack—even an invisible one—quickly becomes uncomfortable. When it does, the student wearing it will likely become disruptive.

Does this excuse misbehavior? No. But it does point the way to a positive resolution. As Jesus' representatives, we can show His love by helping our students "drop their load" for awhile when they arrive in our classroom. How? Few of us who teach in the part-time agencies of any congregation have been trained as professional counselors. Still, we can listen. We can accept the feelings of our students. We can show them that we care. In doing so, we can help them know that Jesus loves and cares too.

If you have never taken a short course in listening skills, you might consider taking one. Most community colleges offer classes like this because people in many walks of life (nurses, teachers, lawyers, parents, accountants—virtually anyone who works with people) find the skills helpful, or even essential for their everyday relationships. Or, ask your local librarian to refer you to a good book or two on listening. Then practice with a friend.

Listening to our students helps build a relationship with them. Even if relationships were not so important in Christ's church—even if our Savior had not said, "This is My commandment, that you love one another"—teachers who nurture interpersonal relationships in their classrooms would experience far fewer "discipline problems." Students who believe their teacher likes them and cares about them are less likely to act up. In fact, they are more likely to exert pressure on one another to behave in acceptable ways.

During the first month of school one year, one of my eighth-grade girls gave me no end of headaches. Frustrated and confused, I listened, lectured, scolded, and even called her parents—twice! All to no avail. Then I gave the year's first math test. Jackie failed. When she got the paper back, she started to cry. I pulled her out into the hallway.

(If, based on the examples in this chapter, you've concluded that I spend a lot of time in the hallway with students, it's probably because I do. I avoid confronting and counseling students in front of their classmates. I encourage you to avoid it too. Our goal is to help— not to humiliate—our students.)

I'm sure Jackie expected yet another lecture. Instead, I confessed that while this was her first time taking eighth-grade math, this was my first time teaching it. I told her—in honesty—that her failure was mine as well as hers. I told her that I needed more practice in explaining concepts and in knowing how best to get the ideas across. Could she stay after school for a few minutes the next few days so I could practice explaining? And would she like to take the test again when I finally got it right?

Her answer was yes to both questions. That afternoon during American history two of the boys in the class started whispering and giggling in the back of the room. Without hesitation, Jackie whipped around and said aloud, "Shut up, you guys, Miss Fryar's trying to talk and I wanna hear!"

Because Jesus helped me demonstrate His love, I had been able to turn a potential enemy into a friend. The turnaround hinged on relationship—a personal relationship built on showing care.

Even as I write this, I wonder. I wonder how to build relationships in the part-time agencies of the congregation. I wonder how teachers who meet with their classes for an hour once a week can communicate their care to their kids. And I wonder most of all about some of the practices that have come into common practice in many congregations:

- If teachers "team teach" by pairing up with another adult and trading duties so that they see their students only every other Sunday or every other month, what does that do to relationships that are so essential?

- If Sunday school superintendents or VBS directors set up programs in which one adult teaches the Bible story, another adult leads music, a third adult plans the crafts, and a fourth adult officiates during closing worship, how can relationships develop? How can a child receive Jesus' love from an adult she does not know and with whom she spends—at most—15 minutes per week?

- Can practices that *seem* to make it easier to recruit adult leaders actually be making it harder in the long run? Because these practices make it more difficult to build relationships, might the practices contribute to the behavior problems that tend to make volunteer teachers less willing to serve?

- How can we help ourselves and our fellow teachers catch Christ's vision of "making disciples"? Can we pray for the commitment and joy we need to take up our Savior's cross and follow Him (Matthew 10:38)? Can we invest more time in the lives of others—particularly the children and young people Christ has entrusted to us in His church?

- How can we keep the goal of "making disciples" in mind all the while using our time and energy wisely as good stewards of our own lives and the gifts God has given us for serving others?

Stop for a moment here. Think about how you would finish these open-ended statements. Jot down some of your thoughts before you go on. Then talk your answers over with your pastor, your Sunday school superintendent, your prayer partner, or another mature Christian friend.

When I think about my relationships with my students and the effect those relationships have had on both their discipleship and mine, I thank God that ...

When I think about my relationships with my students and the impact of those relationships on both their discipleship and mine, I would like God to ...

A FINAL, ALL-IMPORTANT QUESTION

Have I done all I can do—proactively—to keep my class on target? Are my expectations reasonable, given the age of my students and the situation in which we find ourselves? What's in each student's "knapsack" today?

Asking those questions can help any teacher create a positive environment in which to maximize time spent on-task with the class. Still, even if you do all of these things with consistency and diligence, problems will arise from time to time. As long as classes in the church continue to enroll sinners, our students will sin— against one another, against us, and against their Lord.

When they do, we need not see their behavior as a personal insult or as proof that we are inadequate or incompetent. Instead, we can see each situation as a "window of opportunity," a chance to practice what we preach and teach about sin and grace. We can ask ourselves, how can I use this incident as a chance to *disciple* this student?

As a first step, we need to find out whether or not the offender knows his or her action was wrong. If Juanita was absent the week you asked the students to come directly into the classroom when they arrive, you need not scold her for playing in the hallway before class. She needs to learn the new rule. If Fredrick's family curses as a matter of course and if Fredrick has never learned the Second Commandment and its meaning, he needs help understanding God's Law, not a reprimand for disobeying it.

A good opening question in a discussion with Juanita might be, "Do you know what you just did?" We might ask Frederick, "Do you know what you just said?"

Think about the chit-chat in the back of the classroom. It really annoys most teachers. It derails our train of thought and distracts the students who have come to learn. This can be an opportunity to pull the offending students aside and talk with them about why we find the behavior disruptive and aggravating. We can express our concern in words like, "Daniel, the Holy Spirit can't work on your heart when you won't listen to His Word. And you are keeping the others around you from listening too." After a clear conversation like this, we can—and should—treat further offenses as sin. They are.

When a student admits committing an offense, we take the next step; we try to determine the offender's attitude toward the sin. We might ask a question like, "What do you think about what you did?" or "Do you think Jesus approves of what you've done?"

If the answer betrays a hard or cold attitude toward the sin, that student needs to hear more Law from us. For example, "Kevin, I'm very concerned about this. You've disobeyed me, but more important, you've disobeyed the Lord. Sin hurts us. It hurts the people around us. In this classroom, we take sin very seriously."

Most often, especially if a caring relationship already exists between student and teacher, a law-based confrontation like this will be enough to bring the student to express remorse and to ask for forgiveness.

At this point, it's sometimes helpful to brainstorm briefly about what the student could have done in the situation instead. Sometimes students genuinely do not understand that there are alternatives to the hurtful behaviors they use to get attention, to express their frustrations, or to protect themselves.

Once a student has confessed the sin to me, I find it most helpful to ask if we can talk to Jesus together. The student prays for forgiveness. In my part of the prayer, I briefly thank the Lord for His death and resurrection for us and for the assurance that because of the cross, He always forgives us.

Then I intercede for the student in words something like these: "And, dear Jesus, please help Shauna next time she's tempted to (lose her temper and hurt someone else). Give her the power she needs to (tell the other person how she feels and ask for help) instead of (hitting). Thank You that You love Shauna so very much, Lord Jesus. Amen." A brief comment regarding the certainty of God's forgiving love can follow the prayer. From that point on, so far as God is concerned, the incident is closed. And we demonstrate that fact by closing the book on it ourselves.

WHAT ABOUT PUNISHMENT?

The Bible says that when God forgives our sins, it's as though He drowns them in the ocean of His forgetfulness (Micah 7:19). The Marianas Trench in the Pacific Ocean is at one point nearly seven miles deep. If you drop a heavy anchor into the water there, it will not yet have touched bottom an hour later! How deep God's grace toward us truly is.

It's one of the central truths of the Christian faith—God does not punish us for our sins. He punished Jesus in our place. A huge part of the process of "making disciples" involves helping God's children understand and believe that. We have a chance to teach that truth in a powerful way every time a student confesses his or her wrong-doing to us. We can model for that student what God's forgiveness and consistent love are all about.

Having said that, we need to remember a parallel truth: Sin sometimes brings unpleasant consequences into our lives. We dare not shield our students from this reality. Someone who breaks a window should pay for the damage. Someone who steals a jacket and then loses it should replace it and ask its owner for forgiveness. Note that in both examples we're talking about making restitution for losses caused by the sinful action, not about enduring some kind of penalty to "pay for" the wrongdoing.

Then too we need to remember that most sin involves broken relationships as well as broken rules. Once a student has asked for God's forgiveness, we may need to help him/her ask other people for forgiveness too.

The process of restoring relationships can intimidate adults, let alone 8- or 10- or 12-year-old children. Your students may need your help, especially at first, in the process of confessing their sins to one another and praying for one another (see James 5:16). Walk through the process with them. Smooth the way as much as you can.

We can, I suppose, force someone to say the words, "I forgive you" to a classmate who has hurt them. But we cannot force anyone truly to forgive anyone else from the heart. Nor will we gain anything if we try. Give those offended the freedom to feel angry or hurt and to say so. Then allow time for the Holy Spirit to produce in them kindness, patience, and a forgiving heart. In some cases you may want to pray with students for just exactly that.

Think About This

How did the adults around you deal with the sins you committed as a child or teenager? Did that impact your view of God in any way? Explain.

Do This

Read the following short story to your class. Then ask what will happen next and what should happen next. (Note: If you teach preschool or kindergarten children, change the offense slightly. For instance, have Harley wreck a picture or clay sculpture RJ worked all morning to make.)

> *Harley stole RJ's new Addidas jacket. He wore it to the mall and spilled hot dog mustard down the front. RJ heard from a friend that Harley was the thief. He walked into the mall just as Harley was coming out, mustard stain and all. If you were Harley, what would you do? If you were RJ what would you do? Suppose these boys both attended the same Sunday school and you were their teacher, what would you do?*

During the discussion, make as few statements as you can. Above all, do not come up with a solution for your group. Simply ask questions and keep asking questions.

If words such as *forgiveness* or *sin* come up, ask the group to define them. Refuse to accept pat answers. Challenge the group to come up with definitions that someone who had never read the Bible could understand.

After the group has come up with their definitions, you might want to press for an explanation of why each matters. Again, don't give answers. Use silence and questions to stimulate their thought. After your class leaves, ask yourself these questions:

- How clearly do my students understand sin? grace? On what do I base my answers?

- What did I learn from this exercise about how my students view their own wrongdoing? their own need for pardon from God and from those whom they hurt?

- What implications do my answers have for how I handle misbehavior in my class in the future?

WHAT'S THE BIG IDEA?

CHANGING THE WORLD
−ONE HEART AT A TIME−

7

The Quiet Revolution

You probably don't view yourself as a revolutionary. Few Sunday or midweek school teachers have serious thoughts of training as a Green Beret. Few VBS teachers or confirmation instructors plan and lead commando raids to topple foreign despots. Still, you may have more in common with the revolutionaries of history than you might think.

A few years ago, Frank Peretti wrote three novels that took the world of Christian publishing by storm. Maybe you read one or more of them. Regardless of whether or not readers liked Peretti's approach, they most certainly recognized his central premise—the church of Jesus Christ is at war. Unseen armies of light and darkness clash over the souls of human beings. Unseen angels and archangels stand toe-to-toe with the forces of hell to oppose Satan and his schemes for God's human creatures. And we—God's people—play a pivotal role in the outcome of individual skirmishes as we give witness to God's love in Christ for us.

Peretti made the smoke and heat of this battle come alive for many of his readers. Still, no one who reads the Scriptures should have found his ideas new. Throughout the Scriptures, the task of carrying out Christ's Great Commission is described in terms of spiritual warfare. While some in our culture object to terms such as "the Church Militant" and to hymns such as "Onward, Christian Soldiers," Christ's people down through history have seen themselves locked in battle.

By our Savior's grace we have been drafted, as it were, into the winning army. We get to take part in bringing the message of His victory over sin, Satan, and death to a world desperate for Good News. A world that is, in fact, dying without the Good News.

THE GATES OF HELL

The kingdom of light clashes with the kingdom of darkness. We already know the final outcome: victory belongs to our Lord and King, Christ Jesus. Remember His promise to His disciples regarding His Gospel?

> *On this rock I will build My church, and the gates of Hades will not overcome it (Matthew 16:18).*

Think of the promise here! Jesus Himself will build the church. Nothing can stop Him. His kingdom will come. His will—His good and gracious will—will be done on earth even as it is in heaven. And the "gates of Hades will not overcome it."

What does that phrase mean? Let's unpack a few of the implications of that promise. First of all, we can see that the church—Christ's people, you and I together, are on the march against hell. Sometimes we can get the impression that it's the other way around, that the church of Jesus Christ is somehow in some kind of holding action. We can feel besieged and on the defensive.

But in the words of Matthew 16:18, our Lord pictures His army attacking Satan's fortress and plundering Satan's stronghold. No "gate" the devil throws up can keep us out. We are on the attack. Led and empowered by Christ, we overtake Satan's forces, remove his armor, and divide up the plunder (see Luke 11:21–23). But what exactly does that mean? What is the "plunder"? What are the "spoils of war" that we hope to gain?

The answer lies in the words of Christ's promise—"I will build My church" (Matthew 16:18). Can you see it? Can you see that holy Christian church, the banner of the cross snapping in the breeze? Can you see yourself standing with that army, standing armed against Satan and poised to rescue the precious souls for whom Christ died? poised to rescue them from Satan's dungeon of death and despair, of meaninglessness and sadness, of pain, misery, and loneliness?

That's what the church of Jesus Christ is about! Our Lord has declared war on the forces of darkness—those forces that hold human beings hostage in their sin and in the fear of death. Our Lord has already paid their ransom. Now He marches with us to snatch from Satan's cold grip the souls for whom He bled and died. Free-

90

dom! That's the message we proclaim. That's the promise, our Lord's promise, to all who believe in Him.

Now, of course, we do not see any of these things with our physical eyes. We do not smell the smoke and blood of battle. Unless we keep in contact with our Commander and His Word, we can easily fall for Satan's lie that peace has broken out; we can simply sit around the campfire swapping war stories while we wait for our discharge papers and the airline ticket home.

Our enemy, you see, is an expert in propaganda. As one century winds to a close and a new century begins, this lie—the idea that the urgency has passed and that Christ's people can sit back on their Lord's laurels to wait for His return—has become Satan's preferred defense.

NO HURRY?

An old story tells of a junior tempter who comes to Satan. He has finished his homework assignment—planning a strategy to bring all the world's people under Satan's control. As he comes before his teacher to report his progress, he grovels and scrapes. He flatters and fawns all over the devil, trying to win his favor.

When he can put off the inevitable no longer, he reveals the answer he has devised. "We'll tell them there is no heaven," he drones. "And then, we'll tell them there is no hell." Satan looks at his protege for a moment. He frowns. Then he slaps the junior demon halfway across hell's Communication Central.

"Fool," the devil scoffs. "That will never work. You'll never convince humans of those things. We will simply tell them this: There is *no hurry.*" As the story goes, the Armies of Darkness rise to their feet and applaud their master's plan.

Undoubtedly the lie that there is no hurry has done great damage among us. Also, it appears that the junior tempter in the story has successfully sold part of his lie. Satan's propaganda machine is even now up and running full tilt in an effort to convince people that hell does not exist. Satan would have us believe that the Judgment Seat of God is either vacant at present or that it is occupied by a dithering old grandfather who has too much tenderness of heart and too much softness of head to dispense true justice.

The Scriptures denounce people who entertain that thought. God says to them, "You thought that I was altogether like you!" (Psalm 50:21 NKJV). We dare not let ourselves be fooled into thinking that God's eternal Court of Justice somehow resembles our own human judicial systems. God must and will punish sin. No excuses will fly in this Supreme Court. The Judge will dismiss all objections, all appeals.

The wages of sin is death. Even now, people all around us are living out that death. They live in the loneliness and uncertainty of not knowing their Savior, not being able to take refuge in Him from the storms of life. They fill their lives with the trinkets of possessions and recreation and wonder why they feel so empty. And, for those outside Christ, for those who do not hide in His cross, the worst is yet to come.

The tabloid media and even many mainstream news programs promote a view that makes life after death look like some kind of extended Carnival cruise. But the Bible flatly states "Man is destined to die once, and after that to face judgment" (Hebrews 9:27). We know this. And yet we can easily find ourselves lulled to sleep by the lie that there is no hurry.

The church of the first century felt the urgency of proclaiming the Gospel; they looked to the clouds, anticipating the trumpet blast that announced their Lord's return. "Today might be the day," they told themselves. While they waited, they worked and witnessed. They wanted to reach as many people as possible with the dynamite message of repentance and faith. With urgency they wanted to share the message of the cross and the love of the Savior they themselves had received.

TWENTY MILLION

This falls under the category "sad but true": After growing up in the church hearing the message of forgiveness of sins through the shed blood of Jesus, we can take our Lord's love for granted. It may be hard for us to understand and impossible to duplicate in our own hearts the newfound joy and the sense of urgency Peter, Paul, Philip, Dorcas, Lydia, and the other first century Christians found in Christ's mission.

Sometimes we may assume that, of course, everyone who grows up in North America knows about Jesus. After all, most people go to church a few times a year, don't they? Most parents see to it that their children get some kind of formal Christian teaching, right? And those children who attend church and Sunday school, of course, hear about Jesus and about the new life He has made possible, right? They understand and believe it, right?

Assumptions like these simply do not line up with reality. Child Evangelism Fellowship estimates that as many as 20,000,000 children in North America have never once heard the Gospel—and that figure does not include young people in their teens! We cannot dispute the idea that children today are more likely to have heard Jesus' name evoked in cursing than in prayer.

In Romans 10:13 the apostle Paul promises, "Everyone who calls on the name of the Lord will be saved." Then Paul goes on (in verse 14) to ask a series of familiar questions:

- "How, then, can they call on the One they have not believed in?"

- "And how can they believe in the One of whom they have not heard?"

- "And how can they hear without someone preaching to them?"

The words translated *someone preaching* carries the idea of "one who proclaims." It refers to pastors, certainly, but also to any of God's people with whom Jesus has entrusted the task of witnessing about the Good News. Sunday school teachers do it. VBS teachers and helpers do it. Confirmation class teachers do it. Those who lead weekday school classes do it.

And unless we do it—unless we proclaim the message, clearly and accurately—how will the young people in our classes hear and believe? Twenty million—20 million!—children need to hear the fundamental truth that Jesus died for their sins, that He was raised to life on the third day, and that through faith in Him we receive forgiveness and an eternal relationship with God. Perhaps one or two of those children will sit in your class the next time you teach. Perhaps one or two of those children live next door or up the street.

Perhaps the Holy Spirit would like to use you as a "proclaimer" of His love in their lives. What a tremendous privilege!

But maybe you feel a bit intimidated by this challenge—a bit (or a lot) unsure of whether or not you can do it. If so, read on. The next few pages will give you some simple, practical tools that will help you not only witness, but catch the adventure and experience the joy of doing that. We will use an acronym to organize these ideas: **SHARE.**

S—SHOW CONCERN

Some parents would never think of darkening the doors of the church themselves, but will send their children to VBS or to a special weekend program that your congregation sponsors. Showing care for these children can provide the opportunity for God to open doors to hearts that would have remained forever locked otherwise. These people may believe that "all the church wants is my money" or "the church is full of hypocrites." They will have trouble finding strings attached—some preconceived hidden agenda—when we show consistent concern for other people's children in Jesus' name.

When children whom you have never met before show up in your classroom, make a special effort to get to know who they are. Tell them—individually—how happy you are that they have come. Even if they are visiting from out of town and you know you will never again see them this side of heaven, do what you can to help them fit in comfortably with the group.

Listen. Listen. Listen. Ask leading questions about pets, school, favorite activities, and so on. Lead, but don't push. Some children will feel conspicuous and uncomfortable if you overdo the interest. Pay attention to cues that say a particular visitor feels safe and eager to continue the conversation or that he/she would prefer to converse with the other students instead.

Watch for chances to communicate—in words and in actions—the message, "This person cares about me and is glad I came."

H—HELP VISITORS FEEL A PART OF THINGS

When I was eight or nine, my family visited the congregation of one of my favorite aunts. My sister and I went to Sunday school. I remember nothing about the room, the lesson, or the teacher. But I do remember the offering—or, rather, the offerings. Plural.

As the worship time began, the teacher passed a very large glass jar from student to student. The jar was filled with pennies. I dropped in the quarter my dad had given me. I remember thinking that this church must have lots of poor families, judging by their weekly offering. After the teacher said a few things, she passed an offering plate. The other children all dropped dimes and quarters into this plate. Having given my quarter earlier, I had no offering to give. I squirmed in my chair. Now I thought the other children would assume *I* came from a poor family, judging by the fact that they brought two offerings, and I brought only one.

The teacher increased my discomfort by explaining that the penny offering had been for missionaries and the offering plate was for the regular offering, or something like that. At any rate, I spent most of the lesson staring at my lonely quarter sitting against the edge of the penny jar looking as out of place as I felt.

In the whole scheme of things, this incident was not World War III. It did not stunt my spiritual growth. I tell it, though, because it illustrates the way even seemingly "little things," the procedures and routines we take so for granted, can impact the overall impression children take away from any particular experience.

I had attended Sunday school regularly for four or five years. Yet I felt flustered and embarrassed when I did not understand a small part of the routine. I wonder, what must visiting children feel when they have no idea what prayer is or even who Jesus is? If they have never stepped inside a church, what must they think about banners or baptismal shells on the bulletin board or even our classroom altar? Why would we have candles and light them? And what is that big black book the teacher reads from?

If things might raise questions in the hearts and minds of visitors, should we change our routines? Probably not. But such questions do imply that all of us—adults and the children who regularly attend—need to act in kindness and sensitivity to the questions our visitors might have. We simply cannot assume *anything*.

We need to help our "regular students" understand this. We need to help them see themselves as hosts and hostesses, as it were, when visitors arrive. We need to talk together on a day when no visitors are present. We need to help our own students glimpse the potential for sharing Christ with other young people who visit. If we adults sometimes forget that not all children know Jesus, our students may be making that mistake too.

Finally, besides being prepared for visitors, we all need to do what we can to bring visitors—to invite children and young people of all ages—to come hear the Gospel. Some congregations use VBS as their major outreach program for neighborhood children. Some congregations begin a preschool for the purpose of touching young families with the Good News. A few congregations think of their Sunday schools as an outreach tool.

Still, the statistics tell us that we could do more. Millions and millions of children need to know Jesus' love. Our own children need to see that the church does not exist as an end unto itself but as the army of the living God. We are engaged in the serious and exciting business of rescuing priceless human souls from the grip of hell. What better way to meet both needs than to enlist our students as agents of Christ's light? They can invite their neighborhood friends. They can pray for unchurched classmates in school. They can welcome visitors and help put them at ease. Our students can do this—if we lead them into these opportunities.

A—ASK ABOUT CHRIST

Perhaps you come out of a background in which children receive Baptism in infancy and then simply grow up in the church. You may not remember a time when we had to worry or wonder about God's love and forgiveness. You just grew up knowing it, from little on. What a blessing! I would not trade such a blessing for all the world. But as we work with children who do not share this advantage, we need to rethink our methods, our assumptions, and perhaps even our attitudes. We may have to adjust all three. At least a bit.

We've already mentioned the assumption that all children who grow up in North America (or at least in our part of the continent) know Jesus as their Savior. And we've pointed out some statistics to the contrary—startling statistics, I think. How can we find out if the particular students who sit in our classroom are the norm or the exception? How can we find out if this Sunday's visitor is the norm or the exception?

This may sound simplistic, but we could just simply ask. Remember, of course, that you want visitors to return. Therefore you will want to avoid making them feel uncomfortable by singling them out for some kind of special inquisition. But you and your whole class could probably profit from thinking about and answering a question like, "What do you know about Jesus?" or "What do you think about Jesus?" or "Who is Jesus?" or "Why is Jesus important in your life?" You could ask such questions on a regular basis.

Sometime when no visitors are present, walk through a roleplay with your students. Have someone take the part of a visitor who knows absolutely nothing about Jesus. Ask one or more of the questions above and let the students answer them. Then practice, together, talking with the "visitor."

R—RELATE THE FACTS

We've said it again and again in this book. The facts of history matter to Christianity. Our faith is rooted in the soil of actual events and actual people—events and people from a real time and in a real place. This has far-reaching implications for us as we witness to children who don't know Jesus.

Certainly our teaching cannot consist only of the repetition of pious platitudes like "God loves you." Our teaching must go beyond that to other truths. We must help our students know, for example, that Jesus Christ, who was crucified for our sins and raised to life, brings us peace. This content must be expressed and explained in age-appropriate ways.

Should a congregation provide separate classes for neighborhood visitors and students new to the Christian faith, or should instruction take place in the context of established classes? We cannot give a universal answer to this question. But we should ask the question. Then our congregation—and perhaps the individual educational agencies within our congregation—needs to answer the question in a way that fits our situation.

Perhaps God has blessed your congregation with a member whose heart burns with zeal for reaching children and young people with the Gospel. Perhaps you have several visitors of about the same age each week. Perhaps you have a classroom or office vacant during Sunday school or VBS. Or maybe you could use a few more teachers and have already drafted your church's child-outreach specialist. Maybe you've had to plot and plan for weeks as you allocated every square inch of available teaching space. And maybe you have visitors from a wide range of ages and interests.

As you think about the possibilities open to you, pray. Ask the Lord's direction. Then act, based on what seems feasible. As you think through your decision, though, keep these factors in mind:

- Separating visitors may create the impression (with them and with those who regularly attend) that somehow the visitors are "less than"; less worthy than, less smart than, or even less welcome than the others.

- Separating visitors could leave teachers with the idea that their students have progressed "beyond the cross," that their students already "know that story" and therefore they need not return to the basics of Law and Gospel, sin and grace, each week. We've already seen that the question, "Where is the cross?" must be asked and thoroughly answered *each class period* if the students and teacher are to grow in their Christian lives. (See chapter 5.)

- Separating visitors can create within teachers the temptation to rely on jargon—on "church words"—rather than putting the truths of the faith into language all their students can understand. This is not to put down precise theological vocabulary. Words such as "Savior," "justification," and "forgiveness," have beautiful and distinct meaning. But unless and until we have thoroughly explained words like these and our students have grasped their meaning, we can easily find ourselves talking over the students' heads. They may be able to throw around the jargon too. In the process they may effectively disguise the fact that they do not understand the concepts behind the words.

- Separating visitors can give teachers a chance to work with smaller groups of students. Usually that will open up more opportunities for feedback; you can ask each individual to explain specific facts or concepts in his or her own words.

- Separating visitors gives teachers more opportunities to focus the discussion and the message on the specific needs of individuals. It may be easier to help each individual feel welcome and accepted.

- Separating visitors can allow the regular class members to continue into the next scheduled lesson rather than stopping midstream to take another look at what Hebrews 6 calls "the elementary teachings."

Sensitive teachers, pastors, directors, and superintendents need to weigh all these factors. On the one hand, we must remember that the faith involves much more than knowing facts. All of us—children too—need to hear again and again the message of the cross, of who Jesus is and what He has done for us. On the other hand, a class that spends all its time on the ABC's every week will never get into other important aspects of daily Christian living.

One last point. If you do decide to set aside a separate class for visitors or for those who know little about the Christian faith, look hard and long at the question of reintegration. When will these students join their peers? How can everyone feel comfortable when that happens? Probably no introductory class for newcomers should last longer than three to five sessions.

E—EXPRESS YOUR FAITH

We began this chapter talking about revolution, about the warfare in which the church of Jesus Christ finds itself engaged and the sure and certain victory we have in Him. That message revolutionizes human lives. As individual hearts change, so do individual families. Little by little, churches and communities change. No humanly designed plan transforms society. Yet, one heart at a time, one life at a time has changed. Jesus described the same kind of phenomenon when He said, "The kingdom of heaven is like yeast that a woman took and mixed into a large amount of flour until it worked all through the dough" (Matthew 13:33).

We share the facts of what Christ has done. We share what the New Testament so often refers to as *the faith,* the one, holy Christian faith once delivered to the saints (Jude 3). But we also follow our Lord's instructions to the man whom He freed from the misery of demon possession. "Go home to your family," Jesus told him, "and tell them how much the Lord has done for *you,* and how He has had mercy on *you* (Mark 5:19, emphasis added). We share *the* faith, and we share *our* faith.

Led by the Holy Spirit, our witness in the classroom or elsewhere will seldom take the "Dragnet" approach ("just the facts, ma'am"). We will share what Jesus means to us—to us personally and what He's done for us—for us personally. We can provide opportunities in class for everyone to do that kind of personal sharing. For example:

- Jesus helped these disciples in a violent storm. Tell about a time Jesus helped you in danger.

- Paul and Silas prayed in prison and sang praises to God. When have you praised God during a hard time in your life? What did you say?

- Rhoda and the other Christians prayed for Peter's release from prison. God answered their prayer. Tell about a time God answered a prayer for you.

We can lead our students into the habits of daily witness too by modeling that kind of witness for them. It need be nothing complicated. Simple sentences of assurance and comfort can become part of our conversation. For instance:

- "I'm sorry you're hurting so much. I will pray for you."

- "I care about you, and so does Jesus."

- "Wow! What fantastic things the Lord is doing for you!"

- "Isn't God good?"

INVOLVE STUDENTS IN OUTREACH

When I taught on a daily basis, nothing seemed to bring home this notion of the outreach mission of the church more than my reporting to the class the details of specific evangelism calls. For a while one of my classes served as my "prayer partner." Each Wednesday I would tell them what had gone on the night before—regardless of whether anyone on the calling teams even got to talk with anyone.

A number of adults from the congregation thought it an honor to spend one night each week taking the message of the cross door to door in our neighborhood. This fact alone helped my students see themselves and Christ's church in a different light. By praying, they took a real part in the great missionary work of our Lord Jesus—that quiet, one-heart-at-a-time work that revolutionizes human lives. This experience transformed my class members' view of life's purpose.

If you serve as an evangelism caller, by all means share your experiences with your students. If you are not a caller, think about asking to ride along with one of your congregation's calling teams once or twice. Weave your experiences into your lesson plans. Help your students see a bigger picture of the Church Militant.

If you teach older students—perhaps from fifth grade on up—talk with your pastor about whether they themselves could ride along on calls or walk along to help with a neighborhood canvas. Be careful to pair young people with adults who want them to be involved. Pray together before the experience and debrief afterward: What happened? What did the Lord show them? What did He do for them? What did He let them do? How did it feel? Would they do it again? Why or why not?

Think About This

In what ways is the Lord Jesus using you right now to bring His "quiet revolution" into someone's heart or to expand the influence of that revolution still further in their lives?

Do This

Choose one idea from this chapter and introduce it to your class this week. As you evaluate the activity after class ask yourself questions like:

- How was this class time different, if at all, from what we usually do together? If different, was the difference due to this activity?

- In what other ways could I lead my students into more intentional witness in their daily lives?

- What would I like to say to the Lord Jesus about this whole topic of Christian witness?

WHAT'S THE BIG IDEA?

COLLABORATE! NEGOTIATE!
FACILITATE!

Team Works!

Collaborate! Negotiate! Facilitate! Does that sound like a slogan that might come from the cheerleading squad at I Q High? These three words sum up the essence of this chapter. In words of (mostly) one syllable the idea might be stated, "All of us are smarter than one of us." Together, those on the disciple-making team at your congregation can have a much more profound impact on the hearts and lives of your students than any one person who tries to go it alone. Let's look at each of these ideas in the next few pages.

COLLABORATE!

In the old children's story "Stone Soup," a stranger in rags appears in a rural village populated by greedy, selfish folks. Perhaps you recall how these villagers give the stranger a cold shoulder. Then they go home to hide the contents of their pantries so they can plead poverty in case he asks for something to eat.

As the stranger chats with a villager, he drops a comment to the effect that he knows how to make excellent soup from stones. The people are astonished at the claim and anxious to learn the mystery of such a miraculous and abundant source of food. One villager rushes home to gather up a pot, some water, and a cooking kettle. Soon a curious crowd gathers to watch the water boil and to learn how to select "soup stones" that are just right.

Choosing one with a flourish after agonizing moments of deliberation, the stranger remarks, "This stone will make excellent soup—but ah, how much more wonderful it would taste had I a few carrots to add." Eager to learn the best stone-soup-making tricks, two villagers go home, find bunches of carrots they have been hoarding, and bring them to the stranger. He cleans them and puts them into the kettle.

So it goes, as the stranger drops hints and the villagers bring onions, potatoes, stew meat—all the ingredients needed to make a fine "stone soup." When everything has been added and the soup has simmered, everyone in the village agrees that they've never tasted such delicious soup. They will probably turn stone soup into a frequent village feast. The stranger smiles and departs, happy and with a full stomach.

What do you "bring to the table" in your congregation? I have never known a teacher in the part-time agencies of the church who acted anything like the stingy villagers of stone soup fame. But I have known teachers who let themselves be fooled by Satan and by their own sinful nature into thinking that they had little or nothing to contribute to the staff on which they served. I've felt that way myself sometimes. Have you?

But how untrue! God has given gifts to you and me. Each of us has a unique mix of talents, abilities, and experiences. Our Lord is not wasteful; He wants to use you and me—all of what He has given us—for His purposes. He wants to give you and me, each of us, as His gift to others. We serve not just our students, but also those who teach and serve alongside us.

As I sat eating my hotcakes and sipping my coffee at a fast food restaurant this morning, a stranger came up and asked if he could sit down. This happens to me occasionally, because I use breakfast time as my time for my personal devotions. People who pass my table sometimes notice my open Bible and stop to ask a question or to chat. It has led to some interesting conversations.

This morning, the stranger pulled out a chair and asked, "Well, what's the Good News for today?" Because my devotion came from Romans 5, I answered, "Jesus died for your sins and you have a future full of hope."

He smiled and we began a conversation about God's grace in Christ that lasted about 15 minutes. I enjoyed his insights and appreciated his enthusiasm. I left the restaurant confident I had met a brother in the Lord. We may never see one another again until we meet before God's throne in glory. Still, I found myself encouraged as I flipped on the computer and began to write this chapter. I trust he went on his way to work encouraged too.

That's precisely what our Savior intends for His family: that we "encourage one another and build each other up" (1 Thessalonians 5:11). That encouragement happens as we share His Word, His promises, His love, His compassion, and His forgiveness with one another.

Teaching, especially teaching God's Word in the part-time agencies of the congregation, can turn into a lonely business. Everyone on the staff can find him- or herself rushing to get to class after the worship service or vice versa. If we teach midweek class or confirmation instruction, we may *be* the entire staff. Or we may rush from the supper table to get to class or from class to start supper. We would encourage our fellow teachers, we truly would, if we ever saw them!

Isolation brought about by circumstances can numb our zeal. It can blind us to our disciple-making task. It can deafen us to our Savior's transforming Word of grace. Then we can find ourselves demoralized. We may wake up to find ourselves simply going through the motions in class. We may find ourselves aiming no higher than mere crowd control and "covering the material." We may lose our vision for nurturing the faith of our students. The "soup" we cook up for our class may taste as watery as broth made with stones—and carry as many spiritual nutrients.

Collaboration—working together to help and encourage one another—is not an option for Christian teachers. We share

- our faith;

- our ideas;

- our encouragement;

- our equipment and supplies;

- our needs and prayer requests;

- our time and effort.

When we collaborate, we multiply our enthusiasm and the potential results of our efforts. When we collaborate, we divide the burden and the workload. Our Lord made teamwork a hallmark of His own earthly ministry. The Holy Spirit reminds us again and again in His Word of the fact that in Christ's body the eyes need the hands, the feet need the nose. Godly wisdom leads us to conclude that we need to work together.

Suppose. you find yourself on a staff where everyone is friendly—but always in a hurry? What if you find staff relationships good, but you'd like to see them even better? Or what if you find yourself on a staff of "lone rangers," a staff on which each member sends a clear, don't-bother-me message? Here are some suggestions.

- Become a "subversive" for a quiet teamwork revolution on your staff. Begin with yourself. Look for good things happening in the classrooms of colleagues and praise them—with sincerity.

- Start small. Choose one person, probably the one who seems to you most approachable. Make it a point to stop for brief conversation before or after class. Ask how things are going in that person's class. Offer encouragement.

- Stop commenting on the weather. Comment instead on a point drawn from the pastor's sermon or a truth from today's lesson that helped you in your own faith-walk. Use such comments to begin conversations with fellow teachers about your common faith. Look for ways to build up other staff members.

- Ask your pastor or education committee to initiate staff meetings that go beyond the details of this year's Christmas service. If staff meetings do not already include Bible study and prayer, ask your staff leader to introduce them.

- Take some deliberate risks in staff meetings. Ask for help with a specific problem (without mentioning student or family names). Make a specific prayer request. If you let yourself be vulnerable, others will likely follow.

- Have something to share at staff meetings or at other times when you chat before or after class. Choose something positive—an idea from a teaching magazine or book, a truth from your personal Bible study today, an answered prayer.

- Offer to help colleagues. Ask what you can pray about for them or for their class. Suggest combining your class with another teacher's group for a special project (e.g., puppet play, worship time). Let others know when you have extra craft supplies they could use.

NEGOTIATE!

Henry Ford once told an employee who had come to him with a complaint about another worker, "Don't find fault, find a solution." Great advice for team players! It sounds a lot like what the apostle Paul wrote to the believers in Galatia:

> The entire law is summed up in a single command: "Love your neighbor as yourself." If you keep on biting and devouring each other, watch out or you will be destroyed by each other (Galatians 5:14–15).

In every set of working relationships, conflict is inevitable. Every teacher on your staff has a unique way of looking at things, a unique way of doing things. Sometimes their approach to the teaching task, their way of communicating, their need for space or quiet, their educational methodology, or their way of relating to their students will conflict with yours.

Three staff members may want to use the VCR on the same Sunday. Two may have conflicting ideas about classes on Easter. The teacher next door may choose noisy activities three weeks in a row, making it difficult for you to keep your class's attention.

In situations like these, Satan and our own sinful nature can work together to convince us that anyone who disagrees with us is disagreeable. We can fall into the trap of black and white thinking ("I'm right, he's wrong"). We can build walls instead of bridges.

When conflicts arise, we may want to overlook them or ignore them. Many Christians have the mistaken idea that to love means to be "nice" at all times. Don't rock the boat, we tell ourselves. Sometimes this will work—if the problem is small and happens only once. If we recognize circumstances in our own lives that have shortened our fuse for the week, we can adjust to the inconvenience with relative ease. In situations like these, we may choose to follow the apostle Peter's wisdom: "Love covers over a multi-tude of sins" (1 Peter 4:8).

Sometimes, though, we find it impossible to overlook a conflict. The offense or problem may happen again and again. One or more students may be hurt if we do not act. We may find our own hearts hardening toward the person who has hurt us. In any of these cases, we need to take the initiative to "find a solution." Most often, if we take a problem-solving approach to conflict, we can enlist the other person's help—help that person will gladly give.

When we "[speak] the truth in love" (Ephesians 4:15), the Holy Spirit will work with us to bring about a resolution. If I want solution A and you want solution B, He may help us agree on solution C—a solution neither of us thought about before but that is agreeable to both of us. It may even work better for both of us than either A or B would have.

Let's eavesdrop on a conversation that will serve as an example of problem solving. Imagine, for instance, that the person who leads opening worship gradually increases the time for it. Instead of 40 minutes for your lesson you now have 25. Your dialog with the worship leader might go something like this:

You: Wow, Mr. W., my kids really enjoy those new songs you've been teaching them.

Mr. Worship: Thanks. I've found this new book with lots of new worship music. I enjoy it a lot.

You: That's great. I really want my class to learn how to worship from their hearts. I guess that's why I've hesitated to talk to you about something that's been bothering me. I so appreciate what you're doing for the group …

Mr. Worship: Yes, but …?

You: Well, I know how important worship is. I also know how excited I get about teaching my Bible lesson. It seems lately I haven't had all the time I've needed. We haven't been getting back to our classrooms until 8:30, and I'm struggling to fit everything into the half-hour or so that's left.

Mr. Worship: Oh, I guess I've been running a little long on the worship time, huh?

You: Well, the last month or so.

Mr. Worship: I guess I thought no one would care. The kids are involved and enjoying it. I thought you teachers would appreciate the break.

You: I do appreciate what my students are learning from you, Mr. W., and I'm so glad you're willing to lead all of us in worship. But it does present a problem when I plan a lesson and then it doesn't quite fit.

Mr. Worship: I must apologize. I just got carried away on the wave of my own enthusiasm. I'll watch the time more closely from now on.

You: Thanks for listening, Mr. W.

Mr. Worship: No, thank you for telling me. I didn't mean to inconvenience you. Not at all.

Usually an honest conversation like this will strengthen relationships, not damage them—especially if you follow up with genuine words of appreciation and affirmation in the weeks and months that follow. Our words must be heartfelt, not phony. But when they are, they nurture relationships. Adults, like children, appreciate "getting caught doing good."

One final word on negotiation. Problems need to stay between the people who share them. We don't talk to Mr. X about the problem with Mr. W. We don't even talk to the pastor about the problem with Mr. W., unless Mr. W. refuses to listen to us and makes it plain he has no intention of changing his approach. Even then, we will talk to him two or three times before we widen the circle.

I once heard someone explain the difference between gossip and problem solving. It went something like this: *If I am part of the problem or part of the solution, I may in good conscience talk to you about the conflict. If I am not part of the problem or part of the solution, telling you about it is gossip.* That definition rings true to what our Lord Jesus describes for us in His teaching on conflict resolution in Matthew 18.

Probably nothing destroys a staff team more quickly than backbiting. When we complain about another staff person, when we see ourselves as (even slightly) superior to someone else on the staff, or when we gossip about another staff member, collaboration flies out the window. We damage our own hearts and our own relationship with our Lord. We hurt those who hear us. We hurt the person we have complained about.

Still, none of us serves on a perfect staff. Not one of the people with whom you teach has wings or a halo. Honest disagreements will sometimes arise. Sometimes you or a colleague will act in disagreeable ways. Pray for each other and with each other. Expect that conflicts will arise. Take care of today's problems today. Don't wait for them to escalate into a major battle. Don't find fault; find solutions.

Your Substitute Will Love You!

The person who takes over for you the morning you wake up with the flu or the weekend you need to be out of town on business is part of the staff team too. If you take a few minutes to plan ahead as each year or term begins, you can help to make that person's time with your class a joy rather than a possible nightmare.

- Create a file folder or a small box. Put your name on it and let your superintendent or the person who teaches next door to you know where it is.

- In the folder or box place a class list with first and last names of each student. If possible, designate one or two responsible students to whom your sub can direct questions in your absence.

- Include the schedule you follow. Include activities both in and out of the room, the time each takes place, and the person in charge.

- If you have developed a list of class rules, include them in your packet, along with any exceptions you may allow. Also list privileges or responsibilities the students have (e.g., the person with a birthday this week may light the candles on the classroom altar).

- Explain where you store your teachers guide and/or any student materials (not just books, but extra pencils, chalk, erasers, marking pens, art supplies, and so on).

- Include a note card or two with games or art activities the students enjoy doing. Explain how the game is played or the activities work. Also tell where to find any necessary equipment.

- If you've placed ideas for a substitute in a box, and if you occasionally bring treats for the class, tuck in a sealed package of cookies and some napkins into the box. Invite your sub to reward helpful behavior, to give prizes for completed projects, and in general to create good will. (Extra Bonus: Since you will want the cookies to remain fresh, replace the package of cookies every few months. "Retire" the previous package by hosting a "cookie party" yourself.)

FACILITATE!

- If we want to teach for change, for transformation ...

- If we want to teach with the goal that our students will be "conformed to the image of Christ," resembling their Savior in character more and more fully ...

- If we want God's Word to take root deep in the hearts of each student and to make a difference not just for now, but for the rest of their lives and for eternity ...

Then we need to face one fact head-on: we can't do it alone. We must enlist help—from the families of our students and from our church family, the worshiping family of God in which we serve.

Take another look at God's goals for His people—the faith, fact, attitude, and action goals we studied as we began way back in chapter 1. Look at the people to whom God gave the primary responsibility for seeing to it that those goals came to life in the lives of His children:

> He decreed statutes for Jacob and established the law in Israel, which He commanded our forefathers to teach their children, so the next generation would know them, even the children yet to be born, and they in turn would tell their children (Psalm 78:5–6).

Parents carry the primary responsibility for nurturing the Christian faith of their children. God has put you in a unique position to help parents do that. Quite often young moms and dads would like more than anything else to help their children know and love Jesus. But they just don't know how.

Other children live in homes in which Mom or Dad or both have only a nominal faith, where the family attends worship services only a few times a year, where even meal prayers have not become part of the family routine. In either case, a few "little things" you may do can make such a huge impact. For instance:

- Make yourself visible and available. Arrive a few minutes early. Talk with family members who arrive to drop off their children. Don't make a beeline for the door the moment the class session ends. Stick around and stay visible so parents and other caregivers get to know you and trust they can talk to you.

- Choose a curriculum that includes take-home materials, especially materials intended to help families learn to talk about the Christian faith with one another and live out specific aspects of that faith together.

- Express appreciation to family members for what they do and for the faith growth you see in their child. People will know if you're phony or trying to fake it, so say only what you can say with integrity. But do look for the good—you'll probably find it! Whether you see family members in person or call them on the phone, use words like, "Thanks for taking time to come today; I know it means a lot to Percival," or "It's so kind of you to spend your Saturday afternoon with our class on this picnic," or "I just want you to know how much I appreciate the way Esmarelda so often volunteers to pray in class. She's a blessing to the whole group."

- Duplicate a letter for all the families in the class and send it home once each month or so. Address it inclusively enough; remember some families have only one parent living at home, some students live with Grandma or with an aunt, and so on. Explain briefly what you're learning in class. Suggest simple meal or bedtime prayers appropriate for families with children of various ages. Describe simple projects adults and children can do together (e.g., collect canned food; pray for the missionary your class has adopted; earn some extra money and buy underwear or personal toiletry items for a homeless shelter). Encourage parents to call you with questions or suggestions.

- As each new year or term begins, prepare a "Getting to Know You" packet for families. Have your students take these home the first day or first week. Include two or three questions for families to discuss with one another and answer in writing so you can get to know them better (e.g., What do you like to do together as a group? What does Jesus mean in your life? What two things have you laughed about together this week?). Ask them to send a photo of the family to class with their child. Arrange family photos in a display under a title like "God Bless Our Family" or "Daring Disciples." Include a card in the packet they can com-

115

plete with information you will need (e.g., home phone number, best time to call, medical information you should know about, grade in school, interests and hobbies, home church—if applicable). If you plan to serve snacks at any time, you should also ask about any food allergies.

- Invite. Invite. Invite. Plan events, big and small, to which you can invite whole families. Let your students demonstrate what they have been learning. Get the parents or other caregivers to participate with their children in some way (e.g., listen to memory work, work together on a project, create a skit to present). Don't wait for the whole Sunday school or midweek school to do it with you; plan some activities just for your class.

- Call families when children miss class. Speak briefly with both the student and with an adult. Tell the students you missed them. Ask what you can ask Jesus to do for them in the next week. Take the opportunity to express to the adult your care and concern for the student.

- Pray for your students and for their families. Ask the Holy Spirit to guide parents as they disciple their children at home. Ask that He would make adults and children eager to learn His Word and to live out their faith in their daily lives.

Besides enlisting parents and other caregivers in the disciple-making task, recruit your whole congregation. Work together with others on your staff to let everyone in your church know what's happening in the part-time Christian education agencies.

- Ask if you might reserve a page of your congregation's monthly newsletter. Use your space to explain your program. Do it in an eye-catching way. Talk about special events. Focus on people. Name names. Use headlines designed to draw attention to themselves (e.g., "Man Swallowed by Fish"; "Fourth Graders Slay Goliath"; "Longest Memory Passage of the Year"). Let your students suggest articles and headlines sometimes.

- Link worship in VBS, Sunday school, and midweek class to the Sunday morning worship service. Evaluate your worship times in class to see whether or not they reflect the worship life of the whole faith community. If not, do what you can to connect them.

- Teach liturgical responses or other predictable parts of the service. Explain their meaning to your students. The more young people can participate in the worship service, the more welcome they will feel in God's house.

- Encourage your pastor or congregation's worship committee to choose a "hymn of the month." Then teach it to your students so they can sing it meaningfully in church. Some students may even be able to memorize a stanza or two.

- Use verses from the psalm of the week or one of the other readings as memory work for older students. Explain what it means. Urge students to listen for it and to figure out why it fits into the service where it does.

- Help your class prepare a song or skit or a special reading. Ask the pastor or worship committee what might be helpful and appreciated. Practice thoroughly. Be sure the microphones and other equipment will work well.

- Work with your pastor and elders to find ways to involve families with children in the Sunday morning worship experience in a servant-oriented way. For instance, could families serve as greeters? Could they help distribute bulletins?

- Speak up for families with young children. Urge parents to sit in front where their children can see. Work with the youth group or ladies' guild to create "Pew Paks." Include paper, pencils, and perhaps two or three crayons. Encourage parents to let their younger children use these during the sermon. Encourage older students and adults to listen for a key "word for the day" or a key phrase. Print this word or phrase in the bulletin, and encourage everyone to listen for it and note its significance.

Think About This

Ask yourself, "How well do I collaborate? negotiate? facilitate? What grade would you give yourself in each area if you were to fill out a grade card? Write each grade below. Add two or three sentences to back up the grade you chose.

Collaboration

Negotiation

Facilitation

Do This

Choose one idea from this chapter and put it into action this week. Notice: How does this affect the way I see myself as a teacher? How does it seem to affect others on my staff?

WHAT'S THE BIG IDEA?

GOD'S FAITHFULNESS

9

How to Measure Success

A few years ago, a car company adopted this simple slogan: *We are driven!* The slogan, of course, carried a double meaning. It drew attention to the product. Also, the manufacturer wanted us to believe that an attitude of excellence had gone into the production process.

Are you driven? Do you have an ideal, a vision for your students and for their spiritual growth? Do you have an ideal, a vision for yourself, for your own spiritual growth, for the service you give others in the name of Jesus Christ?

What *Is* Success?

Auto manufacturers might measure their performance in one of several ways. They might note how many fenders fall off as their vehicles leave the new car lot. They might count the number of their vehicles still on the road five, 10, or 20 years later. They might keep a record of initial sales. They might pay close attention to the comments on written surveys six months after the sale. Probably most use a combination of several of these factors as they make their judgments.

Public school teachers and boards find it harder to measure educational success. Administrators may keep track of how many students drop out before graduation. They may judge themselves by how many of their students go on to trade schools, colleges, or universities. They may look at the scores on this year's math and reading achievement tests. They may consider comments students make on surveys teachers distribute on the last day of class. Proba-

121

bly most educators use a combination of methods, as do auto manufacturers.

Teachers in the part-time agencies of the church have an even more challenging task for evaluating success. We can test students' factual knowledge—either by asking questions orally or by giving some kind of written evaluation. But how do you measure faith? attitudes? actions? And what's the standard against which you place your students' scores to see whether or not they stack up to expectations?

A STICKY WICKET

Auto manufacturers want to evaluate results because they want to sell more product. Math, science, and reading teachers want to learn better ways to help students move into a useful career. They also want to placate parents, school board members, and taxpayers.

But why would teachers in the church want to evaluate themselves and their students? Why would we want to measure our success? Maybe because we want the time our students spend with us to be as meaningful and helpful to them as possible. Maybe because we want to reassure ourselves that the time we spend is well-spent. Certainly we care about our students and we want our Lord's purposes to be realized in their lives.

Christian educators have always struggled with the issue of measuring results. The world around us emphasizes achievement and avoiding failure. Sometimes we do not see their kind of achievement, and we get discouraged. We do not like what's happening (or, what's *not* happening) in our classroom.

Measuring "progress" in discipleship is a sticky wicket. On the one hand, it's not wrong to want to see growth in those whom we serve. We need to take care, though, that we look in the right places and for the right things. If we're looking for evidence of "success," we need to make sure we're defining it as our Lord Jesus would.

WHERE'S THE FRUIT?

Jesus often used parables about fields, seeds, plants, and trees when He pictured Christian growth. Paul picked up this imagery as he defined and explained the fruit of the Spirit in Galatians 5.

Think about what happens when you plant a garden.

- You plant seeds that look dead but which nevertheless have real power—the power of life—within them.

- You almost never see new growth right away; seed takes time to sprout and grow; if you keep digging it up to look for growth, you may kill the plant or at best stunt its development.

- You cannot make the seed sprout; you simply plant it and trust God to provide the growth.

- You get what you plant; bean seeds will never produce pea vines; carrot seeds will never produce corn stalks.

TOP

> **Stop** for a moment here. Think about each statement above. How many similarities can you find between planting a garden and teaching the Christian faith? (For help see Matthew 13:3–23; Mark 4:26–29; Luke 13:6–9; and 1 Corinthians 3:5–9.)

So many things in the kingdom of God run counterclockwise to similar things in the world. The values of Christ's kingdom are almost always just backwards to what people in the culture around us think. There's nothing wrong with wanting to walk out to the garden and spot apples, pears, or figs maturing on the tree. There's nothing wrong with evaluating our approach, our methods, our attitudes, our relationships with our students.

We get ourselves into trouble, though, if we fall for the trap of expecting instant change. We will find ourselves inflated with spiritual pride if we think that we have made possible the changes we see in the lives of our students. We do not make it possible for them to get a good grasp of the facts of the Scriptures, let alone increase their faith or work changes in their attitudes or their actions. If we do believe that we are responsible for bringing about spiritual growth in our students, we are setting ourselves up to be popped by the pin of discouragement when that growth doesn't show up right away.

Many wise Christian educators avoid the term *success* altogether. They prefer to speak instead of faithfulness. As those to whom God has given the honor of nurturing the discipleship of others, we teach His powerful Word. We apply His Law in all its severity. We proclaim His Gospel in all its sweetness and power. And then we leave the responsibility for results with Him. We leave *all* the responsibility for results with Him.

As the apostle Paul wrote:

> *I planted the seed, Apollos watered it, but God made it grow (1 Corinthians 3:6).*

That's the core of this chapter's "big idea." God gives the growth. He is faithful to do that. He has promised to work through His Word to do in His people what we cannot do for ourselves. Will our students grow in grace as we teach that strong Word? Absolutely. And we will give all the glory for that growth to the one to whom it rightly belongs—our Lord and Savior.

WHILE WE WAIT

Paul evidently left the results for his ministry in the Lord's hands. But we can see from his first letter to the congregation in Corinth that he did not just twiddle his thumbs while he waited for the "harvest of righteousness" God had promised. In fact, in every New Testament letter the apostle tells of his prayers for his brothers and sisters in the churches of God. After he had planted the seed of the Word, Paul did indeed fold his hands—but in prayer, not idleness.

It would be difficult to overestimate the importance of the prayers we pray on behalf of our students and their families. Here are some hands-on ideas you can incorporate into your own prayer life and ways you can involve others in providing prayer support for you and for your class:

- Pray Paul's prayers. The Holy Spirit inspired the prayers recorded for us in Paul's epistles; the things the apostle asks God to do are undoubtedly His will for His people. Use these prayers, inserting your own name and the names of individual students. My personal favorite is Colossians 1:9–12. See also, for example, Ephesians 3:14–21, 6:18–20, and Philippians 1:3–11.

- Create seven brief prayer lists, one for each day of the week. List a few of your students each day, one or two fellow teachers, a few families, and a different part of the next lesson you will teach (e.g., worship, application). Then pray through each list on the appropriate day.

- Reserve a time each class session for prayer. Stand or sit in a circle. Pass a small wooden cross or another fairly durable item from person to person. Tell the students that the person holding the item will be the one praying aloud. The rest of you can pray silently in your hearts. (Make sure everyone in the group knows we can "think" our prayers in silence to God.) After the students feel comfortable completing tightly structured, one-sentence prayers (e.g., "Thank You, God, for _____") move toward less structure. Eventually, your group can pray "popcorn" prayers, in which individuals pray spontaneously around the circle, taking turns as prayer thoughts come to their minds.

- Draw names for prayer partners each month. Put your name in the drawing too. Encourage the students to let one another know about specific prayer needs and praises (e.g., this week's math test, Mom getting home from the hospital).

- Keep a class prayer journal. Record the specific things for which you pray. Record God's answers when they come, including answers in which God's answer was quite different from the answer you expected. Talk together about the way the Lord has kept His promises to hear and answer our prayers.

- After you have used a class prayer journal for a while, help the students make personal prayer journals where they record requests and God's responses. Encourage the students to remember to thank and praise God as well as asking Him for things. Also encourage them to pray for you and for each other.

NOW WHAT?

We have seen who we by God's grace have become. We are disciples of the living Christ, discipled by Him and set apart by Him for the honor of discipling others.

We have seen His goal for us and for our students. He desires nothing less than total transformation into complete Christ-likeness!

We have seen the tool He has given us to use as we go about our teaching tasks as catalysts in His process of transformation. We use His powerful Word.

We have explored ways to communicate that Word during class time and also more informally as we relate to our students, to their families, and as we work with our brothers and sisters in our local congregation.

Finally, as we have seen in this chapter, we can come to our Lord any time with any challenge to ask His help, His guidance, His counsel. He will give it, gladly and freely.

Best of all, when we fail to fully represent our Lord Jesus in our words or in our actions, we have seen that we can count on His unfailing grace and forgiveness.

Knowing all this and relying on it frees us. It frees us to care about our kids, to care about our colleagues. It frees us to speak the truth in love. It frees us to try new methods, to explore new ways to communicate the precious Gospel. It frees us to set goals and to plan lessons designed to teach not just the facts, but to get at those all important issues of faith, of attitudes, and of actions.

One chapter in this book began by comparing the time we spend with our students to a journey. Jesus has indeed called us to a journey of faith, a process of becoming—of becoming like Him and of leading others down that path with us. As you travel, I leave you with these words of Martin Luther:

This life, therefore,

is not righteousness

but growth in righteousness,

not health but healing,

not being but becoming,

not rest but exercise;

we are not yet what we shall be,

but we are growing toward it;

the process is not yet finished,

but it is going on;

this is not the end,

but it is the road;

all does not yet gleam in glory,

but all is being purified.

From *Works of Martin Luther*, vol. 3 (Philadelphia: A. J. Holman, 1930), page 31.

Think About This

When are you most easily led by Satan into thinking of yourself as a "failure" in your role as a discipler of others? What words and promises of God help you most during times like that?

Try This

Explain to your students that you've been reading a book to help you be a better teacher. Tell them that one thing you want to do is to remember to pray for them. Let them help you make a prayer reminder.

Give each student a wooden shape (e.g., cross, heart, oval) from a craft store. Let them decorate it with paints, marking pens, sequins, etc. Tie these shapes to a long piece of string, one above the other, and hang it on a wall near the place where you prepare your lesson. Or make a "prayer tree" by pouring plaster of paris into a can or margarine tub; anchor a small tree branch in it. When the plaster dries, tie the shapes to the branch.

Encourage the students to include their name on their shape. They may add some kind of picture or symbol that represents something about them or some special prayer need for which they would like you to continue to pray. Check back with them on a monthly basis to see whether new prayer needs have arisen and whether you can thank God for any answered prayers.

Then notice. What kinds of differences do you see in your own attitudes toward the disciple-making task? What kinds of changes do you see in the attitudes of your students?